AMER ICAN BOY

American Boy
© 2019 S.C. Megale

ISBN 978-1-970071-04-7

Cover design and book design ©John H. Matthews

Edited by S.C. Megale

Published by Bluebullseye Press

AMER ICAN BOY

THE OPIOID CRISIS AND THE SISTER LEFT BEHIND

S.C. MEGALE

With Afterword by Carrie Wilkens, Ph.D
Co-Founder of the Center for Motivation and Change

Dedicated to Mom,

for her American boy.

You are the barracuda

that moves us forward.

I wish I could take your pain away,

but I don't know how.

I'll just love you more each day

until I find

a way.

ONE

It was April when I sat in the middle of Cub Run and considered driving my wheelchair into the rocks the white foam leapt across.

Laziness and complete lack of energy were probably what kept me. So instead, I sat there and was sad. I planned to sit there and be sad for a few hours.

Behind me, on the bridge, heavy footsteps clunked. I considered turning around but didn't. Then the grass behind me rustled.

"Sarah?" a voice said. "Is that you?"

I turned. It was the burly old man I'd given a hug to that one time in the Manassas Battlefield gift shop. He wore a National Parks slouch hat and carried a walking staff with hiking medallions glinting off it. Grey moustache and big, trusting eyes. He calls me Sarah because he never remembers my real name, and I always let him.

I said, "Yes, it is," and donned my acting skills like an energy shield from the video game *Halo*. A jab of pain, along with a memory, zapped through me.

We talked for a minute, and then the old man nodded back at that pathway. "You want to come with me?"

Well, I had planned on just sitting at the stream and being sad actually. But I glanced at the water and said sure, why not.

He walked with a limp and breathed sort of heavy. We passed through woods. He stopped and tugged down a branch of a flowering tree to my height. The leaves sighed. "Smell that," he said. "That's *Amelanchier*."

I buried my nose in it.

After a few minutes of thawing I began pointing to other trees. "What is that?"

"Honey locust."

"Is that birch?"

"Why, that's sycamore, darlin'."

For about three miles we walked, and we discussed the heat, and his first job in the doughnut bakery. He sang some bassy Virginia tune under his breath and then pointed into the marsh. "Over there, see, those're ducks."

Well, I knew *that*.

When we got to discussing the bluebells, the famous

carpet of wildflowers that blooms over our Civil War woods, I told him, "One time, I forged into the flowers and got stuck on a root. My brother had to come tug me out."

"Did he?" He laughed. "And how old is your brother?"

I paused. "How old is he?"

"Mm-hmm."

"He's twenty-six." A beat. "In Heaven."

The man got quiet. I explained a little more. Then he told me his niece died the same way when she was nineteen.

"Her parents. Nothing they could do, honey, she was..."

Those large eyes reddened.

"Laying on the floor. Next to her bed."

The sounds of my parents, screaming and pounding his chest, returned to me. Cold blood stole through me.

"We love each other in this life," the old man said, with sudden fervor, "even though we all go our own paths. Yours is still planned for you. You know that, Sarah."

When our trails parted, the man hugged me tight. He exhaled and I felt the coarse bristles of his whiskers.

I told him I loved him.

"I love you, too, Sarah. I love you, too."

He swallowed hard as he thumped away, down the opposite trail.

I looked ahead at mine.

It was long.

And I'd be alone.

THIRTEEN YEARS EARLIER

Matt hit my wooden sword with his, and mine clanked to the floor.

"It's okay." Matt bumped the side of his sword onto my ribs. "But I would have killed you." He retrieved my fallen weapon and handed it to me. Then he coughed into his arm.

We were both supposed to be in school right now. Tissues lined the floor of the open living room and empty boxes of Mucinex had been crushed under my wheels in acts of war. Being crippled with a neuromuscular disorder that renders me wheelchair-confined and extremely prone to illness, Mom only allowed me near another sick person if I were already infected. Matt and I had stayed up all night in his room for a Sick Sleepover. We sketched pencil portraits of dwarves and blew our noses and talked about Elvish politics in *Lord of the Rings*. He was stronger than me, and five years my senior. Even though his pallor was still a little dull and his eyes hooded, Mom said he would go into school late today. I got to stay home.

But until Mom remembered this fact, we sparred.

"Okay, go," said Matt.

I swung my sword at him. He blocked with almost artistic spins. *Thunk. Thunk. Thunk.*

My eight-year-old face was twisted with intensity. I wanted to impress.

"Nice," said Matt. Almost winded—or maybe he just sniffled. And then I think he'd had enough. He pressed hard against my sword and locked me there. I knew what came next.

Matt flung our swords in a huge arc and mine went soaring. I let go before he broke my wrist.

The weapon clattered to the ground next to our clump of Xbox wires.

Beat. Again. Matt grinned.

His teeth were always straighter than mine, and whiter. His hair was long and curly brown. A loose *The Cure* T-shirt hung from his slight shoulders. He wore puffy Vans shoes with too many laces. Matt was lanky, handsome, symmetrical. The total opposite of my crooked body and unevenly mixed features of Mom and Dad. Matt was all Dad.

But I always thought that maybe there were things that only I noticed. His smooth and long fingers. The birthmark on his shoulder blade. The sloppy way he walked.

That gait mystified me. He was never unbalanced in

the lacrosse or hockey arena, neither of which would be his favorite sport—which he discovered about a year later. As for me, I was down for anything with him. I trailed in his wake through *Warhammer* shops stacked with metallic paint and into neighbors' backyards to steal bamboo. Sometimes those stalks were our swords. He rode the back of my wheelchair into battle several times.

Matt's grin faltered when we heard a creak of someone approaching. Our noise had lured Mom.

He looked at me just before the attempts at persuasion began, hoping to stay home still. Mom picked up crumpled tissues and denied every appeal, including my own, with a knowing chuckle. Her Irish eyes were always bright with the next task at hand or idea to chase. And now I supposed she meant to push one of her eggs off to be scrambled and challenged in the world again. Just not our little world. Matt's face fell.

He didn't say goodbye to me as he trudged upstairs to get ready. All the muscles in his shoulders sagged.

I stayed there in the living room, just the swords and me now, while Mom went to bang pots on the stove for my lunch.

For some reason, my heart was heavy.

Sometimes life for Matt did not seem fair.

TWO

Matt ducked into the car with his board under his arm and slammed the door. He never smelled good after the skate park. He would end up panting and covered in sweat, with holes ripped in his black shoes until he tried rejoining the soles with super glue. Everything to him could be fixed with superglue. Mom used to mutter as she tried to pierce the dried solvent with a sewing needle.

But he grinned. Always he smiled, and especially with a board in his lap. Mom pulled down the sun visor in the minivan and pumped the wheel towards the parking lot exit. She asked him about his day.

The interest began in 2004. Right around Matt's early adolescence and time in junior high. Skateboarding in our upper-middle-class suburban neighborhood wrinkled noses. It was loud, territorial, and competitive. Wheels on cement echoed far. Little funding failed to erect designated parks and spilled exhibitionist skaters into streets, alleys, public stairs, and curbsides. Middle schoolers cruised longboards—the slower, larger cousins—down our quiet streets and caused no such disturbance.

But what fun were they?

Fun attracted my older brother, and he attracted fun. To things that were less fun, he paid no heed. His grades sagged in Stone Middle School, and hit the ocean floor of Westfield High. An early diagnoses of ADHD won him visits to counselors and a few summer make-up classes in the "alternative" high school, the one whose reputation caused lightning and thunder to crack at its very mention.

As I trailed in Matt's wake a few grades behind, however, his former teachers I encountered never reflected frustration. Their eyes glimmered at the same time they shook their heads. Once, in a school play, when Matt was denied the role he wanted as the male lead—Paul Bunyan— he instead insisted on portraying his second choice: the pioneer wife. We have a photo of him marching onstage in a red dress and bonnet. It still brings us joy.

Being just as mischievous as my brother, I never saw the

same undesirability in Matt's new skateboarding crowd that everyone else did. At least not at first. He brought with him to this street sport the same effervescence of the lacrosse field and MMOs (massive multiplayer online games). There's a YouTube video called *Segmentum* put together by his crew—I have no idea what the title means—that's several edited minutes of Matt laughing, launching off half pipes, and soaring over rails through a fisheye lens. He said that if a sponsor only would pick him up, he'd go pro and make a fortune. As long as the sponsorship wasn't from a "poser" like Tony Hawk.

Sad that Matt was slowly leaving our fantasy games and stories behind, I tried to include myself in his new hobby. I watched him glide on his wheels (much smaller than my own, I noticed) in the middle of our street. The sun flashed off hubcaps and headlights parked along the curb.

"Name any trick," Matt said, "and I'll do it."

"Okay..." I thought hard. There weren't many I knew.

"Kickflip," I said.

Matt leapt and flipped his skateboard with a twist of his feet. He landed perfectly, and looked at me, proud.

"Ollie," I said.

"That just means jump." Matt laughed.

"So? Ollie!" It was fun to say.

I tried supporting him with equipment. For Christmas,

Mom, Dad, and Santa would arrange our gifts into piles—Kelley the oldest, Matthew the middle, and Shea the baby. My gift to Matt was a clumpy, heavy lump of wrapping paper. I dropped it in his lap and leaned in as he opened it. Two hunks of metal tumbled into his hands. I had gotten him what I thought was the randomest piece of skating equipment I could find: trucks. The steel connectors between board and wheel.

Matt's laugh seemed sincere. "Thanks, Birdie." His nickname for me. "I actually really needed these." But I don't know if he really did.

His clothing became baggier and rattier despite the UVA shirts and khaki shorts hanging in his closet. His pants started to droop intentionally to reveal the top of his plaid boxers. His hair grew longer and curlier. He was getting thinner. Even his music was roughening. He went from *Linkin Park* to *Tupac* and *Eminem*. Soon I was trying to compete in his rap battles in the basement. I started to feel like I could never keep up my end of the friendship.

None of that, in itself, should spawn judgment. None of that would have mattered if it weren't for the smell that began to cling to him soon after, when he returned from a skate spot in DC or a sleepover with friends. It wasn't the gritty, bitter scent of tobacco — the only way I could describe this smell at the time was *funny*. A *funny* odor lingered on him.

My parents will say that this was the turning point.

Not to me.

I can pinpoint that transformative moment; the night and the place I was stunned to not recognize my best friend when I looked at my brother.

I can pinpoint it in two words: *Fuck you.*

Fuck. You.

I slap these words around now. They're punctuations of my writing. When someone pisses me off they replenish in my mind faster than Little Caesar's shovels those mini pizzas onto food court stands.

But in our house, when all three children were under sixteen years old, those words were never uttered.

It was night. Late. The television flickered blue light onto the couch because it was stuck on input. My brother and sister had been fighting, and I'd retreated farther back into a corner of the living room with my folder of Ancient Egypt homework. Matt sat on the couch, both knees drawn up on it. Kelley stood. She was confronting him on hearsay in the school about him, hearsay I didn't know about.

Suddenly Matt snarled the words at Kelley.

"FUCK you."

Silence.

Matt glared at her. She stared back in shock. And then

she bolted for Dad.

By the front door, I heard her yell in tears what Matt had said. And our normally gentle, demure father came storming in. The floorboards nearly shuddered.

I couldn't retreat any farther into my corner.

"What did you say to her?" Dad was in Matt's face. Matt refused to look at him. "Huh?!" Dad shook.

My father never raised a hand in response to our own violence, and little did I know how familiar the trembling of restraint in Dad's muscles in the face of my brother would become to me. When Matt refused to speak, Dad jerked away and spat some punishment: the loss of this or that.

But a vibration entered our house that night. I could feel a change from my quiet, frightened corner of the living room.

I had to pass my brother to escape the charged space. In that blue glow from the television, I will never forget what I saw in him.

A face contorted. A brow impossibly low. His hands twined in his hair.

And eyes glaring at the floor.

He wore the anger so darkly and it consumed him so deeply that I felt surely this couldn't be his own. Surely he couldn't belong to it. I had no way to know how wrong I was.

In that moment, I paused to look at him. To see if it was okay. If I should reach for my best friend.

Something told me I couldn't. Something told me I was losing that chance.

THREE

The phone rang in one long, unbroken roll. Kelley picked up.

"Hey, Shea."

I cleared my throat. "Hey, Kel."

"What's up?"

"Nothing much," I said. "I just got your email with suggestions for Matt's book."

"Oh, great! Yeah, they're just some thoughts."

"Yeah…" I was looking at the email as we spoke.

"Did you finish reading it?" she said.

"Not yet. It's a little long."

To be clear. My sister had sent a 4,400-word email.

Each paragraph detailed another wonderful era of

Matt's life: his antics, his humor. The colors that he flooded into the world.

"I don't know if I can fit it all in," I said.

"I know." Kelley's voice was warm and optimistic. Somehow the brutality of the world never seemed able to penetrate her. "I just want everyone to know how funny he was. And how he made *everyone* smile."

"He had a great smile," I said.

"And I remember more than you do," she reminded. It's true. I'm the only one in the family who had four fewer years with him.

"I'll definitely try to fit in the sprinkler story," I said.

Six-year-old Kelley had convinced five-year-old Matt one day to drag the machine-gun-esque sprinkler into the living room of our house while they both squealed with laughter. Water flung onto every picture frame and throw pillow.

"Oh, totally," said Kelley. "And also how he'd call dump trucks *dum fwucks.*"

I chuckled and scrolled to that suggestion in her email.

"I just want to make sure it's natural," I said, "that it won't look forced."

Kelley paused. My words perplexed her. "It's about his life though, isn't it? And his life was more than drugs. We had a normal childhood."

"I know," I said.

"We carved pumpkins at Cox Farms."

"I know."

"And he had two dates to the prom."

"Who does that?" I laughed.

"All of that is important, too," said Kelley. "It's just as important as the dark stuff."

Figure that. Light is as relevant here as dark. I pursed my lips because maybe she was right. Maybe writing about Matt's life wasn't this bleak because of his own darkness.

Maybe I'm giving him some of mine and selling it off as his.

"I'll work it in," I told Kelley. "I'll find a way."

"You'll be great, Shea," she said.

I just have to find a place for it all.

SPRING 2007

I slammed the bucket of Play-Doh on the checkout counter. Candy, crates of Wiffle Balls, and Nerf guns were piled around me. Now was the time when I would have thrown wads of cash at the clerk and made it rain if I could lift my arms that high, but instead I looked up at Melanie.

Melanie was my attendant at the time. College kid, long blonde hair, and full, rosy face. Best hugs on the planet. She passed the clerk a few folded bills given to her by my mother.

We had been at Toys "R" Us for over an hour. I questioned not the unprecedented shopping spree. Mom had simply informed me of this welcome surprise and I followed Melanie out the door, into the van, and to my favorite emporium like I deserved the damn store.

When I rolled into the house afterwards, shopping bags hanging off the handlebars of my wheelchair, the dogs sneezed welcomes and my hand swatted down to pat their heads and accidentally brush an eye or two.

Melanie and Mom said goodbye a little quickly. I'd never heard Melanie's keys jingle so fast into her hands, and the door close so suddenly.

I looked up at Mom.

"Could you sit down with me for a minute?" Mom asked.

My stomach stilled. Slowly I wheeled to the couch, making the wooden ramp into the living room groan. Mom sat, and exhaled shakily.

"Sweetie," she rested a hand on my knee, "we sent Matt away."

I blinked. Mom studied me.

"What?" I said. "Where? What do you mean you *sent him away?*"

"Daddy and I were worried about him," said Mom. She was strong for me. "We sent him to a wilderness rehab in West Virginia."

"Why? What do you mean you *sent him away?!*" I repeated. My tone rose. My muscles stiffened. I grasped the joystick of my wheelchair like I was about to chase after him.

"A rehab came to pick him up while you were gone," said Mom, and now an escaped tear drew a line down her face. "I'm sorry, Shea. It was so hard to do."

"I need to call Dad," I barked. He was with my sister on a school trip. I later learned that if they had canceled it, Matt may have known something was up and tried to resist.

Mom repulsed with surprise. "Are you angry?"

"Yes!"

"Why?" said Mom. She didn't show anger herself, which alarmed me. Her voice was feeble and rocky. It was almost as if she wanted to know if my anger was justified and if she had thus done the wrong thing.

"Because!" I shouted. But I had nothing. "Because! You don't just *send him away!*"

"Honey—"

"Did he even know about it?!"

"No." Mom's face was getting redder. "He was so good though, Shea. He was crying but he went. Oh Shea." A sob. "He was so good."

I fumed over the next few hours. I locked myself away and cried and hit things. Soon that crumbled into sadness and I cried but hit nothing. I hugged Mom.

Over the next few weeks, Matt went through a rehab for troubled teens in the middle of the West Virginia woods. At first was the silence. His anger. No letters.

Later came a beat-up white envelope addressed in squiggly black handwriting. It was to me.

I used to stare at the bedsheets in fear over YouTube videos Matt had shown me which supposedly disproved the existence of God. He'd busied himself with untangling his faith and lack thereof. Before then, doubt had never even occurred to me. So when I received one letter folded against a cross Matt had fashioned out of two blades of grass, I held it in my hand and paused.

I wrote to Matt in my weak, knotted script probably four times. It went several pages.

Remember that I am always holding your hand, Matty.

I know that your little hand is holding me, Matt replied, *I just wouldn't hold on.*

I know where this letter is today. I cannot unearth it.

Finally, to her joy, even Mom got a letter. She'd waited weeks and weeks, writing novels to him almost every day, because even though *parent* doesn't mean *professional* when it comes to managing a drug addicted child, they know how to love their kid. Ripping open Matt's letter with urgency and excitement, Mom unfolded the page and found one pencil-grey word with a smiley face.

Hi ☺

At last the day came when families were invited to complete the final weekend of the retreat with their loved ones. Mom, Dad, Kelley, and I loaded into the van.

We drove west. We drove until traffic lights became branches and tolls tumbled away into leaping brooks. The roads carried us higher into pure skies. I remember inhaling a gallon of air as soon as we parked and banged closed the van doors. It smelled like silt and dandelion seeds.

The counselors greeted us in front of a large log building. It was round, like an enormous yurt. Other families gathered. Some just a set of parents. Others, siblings and grandmothers.

All of us were anxious to see our loved ones, but all were disappointed when we were told *not yet*.

First, we met with the personal counselor assigned to the campers. Matt's was a middle-aged woman, full of love and hipster vibe with woodsy tan clothes and flyway brown hair. But intelligence was behind her words. She discussed Matt's progress and challenges. Then we had group counseling. We learned about the diverse struggles the adolescents were here for.

One cut herself. One was so addicted to an online video game, he stopped eating and tried to commit suicide when the parents took the game away. A pair of siblings both struggled with MS-13. And Matt, my sweet brother: drugs.

When group therapy concluded, we were shepherded into a small room and held our breaths. The lead counselor, a steady-mannered man in a tie-dye shirt named Mike Beswick, turned off the light and told us to wait quietly while the kids were brought in to the room across the wall.

We did.

Bop! Bop!

And boom. Thunder and rain clashed. Hopped. It rose and shook the walls. My face brightened in confusion and joy and I heard Dad chuckle behind me. Beswick opened the door and the volume tripled and as I moved into the open room, I saw it wasn't a storm.

It was drums.

The adolescents formed a wide circle and held *djembes* between their knees. They whacked them with trained hands, the song a choreographed stampede. Half the room pounded bass and the other half slapped the rim of the drums like raising objections. Then they switched.

We family members filed in, necks turning to keep our awe upon our respective loved ones. Native American and oriental banners hung from the walls: rising suns, Buddhist symbols. And there beneath one sat Matthew.

Matt's eyes didn't turn to us, but not out of spite. He watched his drum mates with an open mouth and relaxed posture. His clothes were clean and soft-looking, just a regular solid-color T-shirt and khaki pants. His face clear and healthy. His long hands smacked the skin of the drum in perfect sync.

We found seats and observed the rest of the song.

"Families," said Beswick at the close. His sandy hair was shaggy but short and his eyes were gentle. That tie-dye shirt and sandals contrasted his wise, professional speech. "What did you think?"

"I didn't know if the beat was the drums or my heart," I said, and Matt and my gazes found each other at last. He looked happy.

We learned a lot about Matt in the following days. "All he does is talk about you," his camp mates would say and smile at me. But we learned too that I was a disturbance for him.

"Matt is troubled by Shea," Beswick told us. "He can't reconcile a loving God with her condition and attributes some of his struggle to her disease."

Mom and Dad's expressions tightened at this.

"But Shea can't be the start or the solution to that either," Beswick went on. "A lot of this is himself and his depression. Matt needs purpose. Matt needs to be involved in a community where the problems are bigger than his own."

I never stopped thinking about that last sentence.

A few times before the end, the counselors assigned parents to another person's kids to give guidance and share their stories. Matt was paired with the short, kind-faced Hispanic father, Jorge, of the MS-13 campers. We were paired with the young woman who cut herself. She connected with me over Disney films and at our very last meeting, she sang to me, in front of everyone, *Part of Your World* from *The Little Mermaid*.

The experience was full of healing and discovery, tribe and music. It'd been a long time since I had seen Matt's white grin blind me that often, or seen his feet cross as he leaned against the building and rested a hand at his chin, chuckling. The earth looked beautiful when it was behind him.

Backs were thumped and eyes were closed in the goodbye embraces. Addresses exchanged. Men grunted when loading luggage into trunks—especially the drums.

Every camper, on the dime of the rehab, was allowed to craft and take back with them one large *djembe*, so that they could find a local circle and continue this important sense of belonging.

When Matt revealed his drum to us, he had to haul it forward with both arms wrapped around the top.

It was red, with a blue dragon painted on it. A yellow heart behind the dragon. And a homemade wooden stand used to adapt the instrument so a handicapped person could reach and play it.

The *djembe* had my name on it. Matt had given his one drum to me.

We prepared to take him home now. Nervous, we prepared to start again.

Before coming here, I remember asking Mom, "Are we going to get the old Matt back?"

At the time, I thought she said, "Yes."

Looking back, I think she said, "I hope."

FOUR

I snuck up behind the man and bumped him with the foot rest of my wheelchair. He jumped. He had grey hair, moustache, and the drawling voice of a cynic.

"Get out of here," he said.

"Not until I steal half your shit," I said.

He turned to another patron. "Shove her aside, will ya?"

The patron looked at us, stethoscope in hand, and furrowed his brow.

"Fine," said the man, dead serious. "I'll just stick some of these instruments on and fry you." He sighed, sat on a stool.

We loved each other.

His booth at the antique market was piled with vintage

medical equipment. I loved scouring through the leather boxes and corked bottles of rancid medicine. Throngs of people wove in and out; the general noise was high.

"What's this?" I said.

"Microscope slides."

"How about this?"

"1920s condoms."

"Ooh." I asked the price on that one.

I found myself a glass eye and a tin of quinine. All would look crazy cool on my shelf of relics. But there were two more little boxes I wanted to open. Inside one was a weird, revolving metal thingamabob.

"How much is this?" I said.

He peered at it. "Nah, I'm not selling you that."

"What! Why?"

"I don't even know what it is."

"But it's cool."

"Come back next month when I know. What if it's junk?"

I smirked and shook my head. Grabbed the other box.

I opened it and the smile slipped off my face. I froze.

My fingers pinched what was inside and lifted it out.

A needle point flashed at me. It was an old, personal syringe.

I put it back and slammed the case. Handed it to the vendor.

"I can't do that."

Memories tried to press a pillow against my mouth and nose but I pushed it away. His name tried to form, but I ignored it desperately.

I left the booth. For some reason, my arm started to ache.

TEN YEARS EARLIER

Matt tried heroin for the first time on a night in early September 2007. He was sixteen.

Those same friends he met grinding the concrete of skate parks had joined him in rattling around pills like Percocet and Vicodin. They liked the feeling, but it was child's play, and only a pastime when they could shake out a few capsules from a family member's prescription bottle. They were too broke and too isolated to buy anything besides pot.

They got a call on a Saturday night. Someone they all sorta knew. "Hey, I got some oxytocin if you guys wanna come over and try some for free."

They went.

Here is where I can take these facts and conjure the story in my head. I see my brother thumping down basement stairs in a house he didn't know well. PlayStations blasting and Doritos bags crinkling around. The host, that young man with greater motives, showed Matt and his friends to a low table.

"Here—one, two, three lines. One for each of you," said the host.

Seconds later, my brother and his friends rolled over, conscious but paralyzed. It sickened and squeezed the life out of their bodies so that a millimeter's movement swung vertigo around them and heaved vomit to their throats. "We're gonna throw up," Matt's friend groaned.

"Just stop moving," I can imagine the host suggesting, because when they were still, completely still, the floating, magical feeling worked. It engulfed them deeper and deeper.

The host and his girlfriend acted like nothing was unusual, and at some point in the night, they stirred their three rookies.

"Get up," he said. "We're going to Target."

I have no idea why, but my brother and his friends joined this young man in his car and on a trip to town. That movement spiked up the illness. One threw up out the window. My brother keeled over to do the same as soon as he tried to wobble in the parking lot below that glowing red Target sign. They never made it inside.

There was nothing more to do with these three than drop them off at home. For hours into the night they lay on the lawn, immobile. Matt crawled around the side of the house to vomit again when his friend's father opened the door to investigate. He was shooed away fast.

It wasn't until later that they learned the powder they'd snorted was not oxytocin. It was heroin.

And the host knew it.

Matt's friend, who was with him that night, told me more a decade later. "He [the host] was our friend, yeah. But they were all addicted; [they all] needed to support their habits. They offered extra. They offered lower prices. They all started dealing essentially... It was too much for us."

Knowing he'd taken heroin disturbed Matt. He swore he'd never do it again. So I will never for all that is sacred understand why there was a second time.

The original host had by now hooked handfuls more customers than just Matt. These others convinced my brother and his buddies that the first time is the worst, and by the second time, it's amazing. One in their group was diabetic. How convenient was it that he brought the needles?

Insufflation of heroin is an entirely different experience from injection, they said. My brother's fear of needles gave way to the promise of euphoria.

"I don't remember it happening, but all of the sudden it became an every other day thing, every three day thing, which so quickly became every day," added Matt's friend to me.

What had that wilderness rehab done? It had buffered

Matt's habits for a little less than year between coming home and that fateful night in September. That's all.

I wonder every minute now what I was doing that night Matt staggered over the Target parking lot. It happened under my watch, in my infant adolescence, when computer screens started to draw me and interests in writing and boys started to bud.

I ask for his forgiveness now in the faults I know I have made portraying these events in his life. But I was not there next to him. My brother, my playmate, was no longer at my side.

Except one night, after an explosive fight between Dad, Mom, and Matt. Silence took over after the storm. Mom and Dad sat far apart from each other on the couch and stared into nothing. Fists were clenched.

They'd told Matt to "Just go." I don't remember where to. Matt banged and crashed items into a bag near the front door. I witnessed it all, and all I could feel was sorry. Was love. Was confusion. Why were Mom and Dad being mean to Matt?

He sounded so alone packing at that front door. And they weren't going to him.

In the quiet, I left Mom and Dad and approached my brother.

He looked up at me, stuffing clothes into a bag. His voice was sad.

"Hi, Birdie."

Tears filled my eyes. I moved to him.

I still remember how soft his lint-covered wool hoodie was as I hugged him. He held me.

"Just promise you'll never leave me," I said.

He breathed shakily. But he sounded unsure.

"I won't."

FIVE

I bit the dry erase marker's cap, spat it into my lap, and wrote onto the board. Blue ink gushed onto the slippery whiteboard. The marker was nice and new.

Seventeen sixth graders were behind me in a horseshoe arrangement of desks, trying to read as fast as I wrote. A photo of the young new bishop, wearing purple and black, grinned on the back wall.

At some time in my life, I realized I cared about the Catholic Church and that's why it drove me insane. The more disappointed I was with how its followers prioritized, the more adamant I was about teaching for it. As a catechist, I taught them about Christ, but also humans. I taught about love, but also attraction. I taught about prayer, but also action. Through an anonymous mailbox system, my students felt safe writing to me about bullying, abuse, and even sexuality. One came out to me.

I considered myself a vigilante. A Robin Hood. A quilt with safehouse patterns like in the Underground Railroad.

Today's lesson was "Respecting Life."

The church expected me to stress the "grave mortal sin" of suicide. Instead, I wrote two things on the board. Just two.

Depression is a disease.

Addiction is a disease.

I turned to my class. Their expressions were tight and confused.

"Do ants matter?" I said.

I paced in the center of the horseshoe of desks. In my head, I saw myself as a professor crossing her hands behind her back and twirling the marker. In reality I probably looked like one of those robotic vacuum cleaners patrolling the tile.

Some students shook their heads, others stared at me.

"I don't know," I said. "Do they?"

"Not really," said a student.

"Not really," I repeated. "Hmm."

"I mean they don't make a difference in the long run," another student chimed.

"Nah, probably not," I said. "So I can squish it, right?"

No objections.

"How about two. What if I squished two."

Silence. Now they knew I was going somewhere with this.

"I have the power, right?" I said. "Should I squish two? How about three? Do three ants matter?"

More silence. I turned to the board.

"So ants don't matter. Does *one* person with a disease matter? We have the power to kind of squish them too, don't we?"

"How?" said a tiny voice.

I had to smirk. How many ways can you squish an ant?

"These people suffer enough without our judgment," I said. "They lose friends, futures, end up in jail..."

I heard pencils scratching on paper. I noticed some eyes glazed. I hadn't been talking for more than a minute, but I knew the problem. I addressed it head on.

"Antonio." I turned to the young boy on my left. He looked up from his doodle. "Do prisoners matter?"

"No," he said.

"Why not?"

"They did something bad."

"Have you ever done something bad?"

"Well...yeah."

I gave him a pointed look.

"But they did something bad on purpose."

"Have you ever done something bad on purpose?"

His round face pinkened. "No..."

I smiled. Then looked at the rest of the class. They all smiled too.

"I mean...maybe." He glanced around at his peers.

"I wonder if anyone here has been to prison. Show of hands." I asked the group now. No one raised a hand.

And then, slowly, I raised mine.

Pencils slapped flat on desks. Eyebrows shot up. I had their attentions now.

"I've been through barbed wire fences, metal detectors, pat downs, and one-way glass in five different prisons."

Conversation and gasps exploded. I flagged them down with both hands lest our noise summon the priest. They finally hushed and gazed at me.

"I wasn't there for myself," I said. "I was visiting someone I love."

And as soon as I said the words, I realized I had backed myself into a corner I wasn't prepared to enter. I spun for the board to move on to another topic, but a little voice stopped me. Pain spasmed in my heart, and I froze. It said,

"Who?"

JANUARY 2008

The stove clicked five times and then blue flames burst from the burner. Melanie shuffled out spaghetti into the water.

I perched at the kitchen island with her, but the house was silent. In the living room I could see Mom and Dad sitting on the couch and staring into space. Mom's nose was red and her arms crossed. Dad's hand was curled into the fist again.

Last night, Matt was pulled over by cops. One of his friends betrayed his confidence and tipped off authorities that there were drugs in his car. Indeed there were. And Matt was pushed onto the hood, handcuffed, and protested in tears. The wire his friend had been wearing caught every word.

Somehow my twelve-year-old self took this news without much alarm and with a too-mature sense of calm. Mom taking my hand and sitting on the ottoman didn't soften any blow because there wasn't one. He wasn't dead, he was just arrested.

I was expecting this much.

Nothing, nothing relieved Matt's addiction to heroin. He attended his second rehab, after the wilderness rehab, at a mental ward called Dominion. If dementors from *Harry Potter* existed, they would circle this place. Matt was roomed with schizophrenics, the homicidal and suicidal, and hallucinating of all kinds. He shouted curses and hit walls and demanded he be released. He was kind of right. That place was not him.

His anger and lying grew. Suddenly I would open my desk drawer and realize my ring was gone. One day we came home from a walk through the backyard and saw empty space where our TV once was. Dad rushed to the window to find Matt hauling this boxy, heavy television down the lawn with both hands to a beat-up brown sedan accented in grey spray-paint. When Dad's hand caught his shoulder and spun him to face him, Matt said, "What the fuck are you doing? This is my TV."

The pawn shop in Manassas knew him well.

But Dominion was not Matt.

His instinctive response to being apprehended in a lie was anger. He'd throw things, storm downstairs. More than once I saw fury almost inhuman in his eyes as he would glare at Dad with his chest heaving or clang around the kitchen drawers for a butcher knife. He threatened suicide often.

But Dominion was not Matt.

Neither was prison.

In the courthouse pews were a scattering of other lawyers and scribes. One was a reporter for our local neighborhood newspaper. The reporter was there to write what would be a brisk and uncompassionate article headlined PRISON FOR MATT MEGALE next to FROM MUSIC TO VOLUNTEERING, an article about a sweet old home music tutor retiring to volunteer and spend more time at her favorite yarn shop. Community marriage engagements were announced on the page after. If this sounds like theatre on my part, I'm sure the issue is still online somewhere in PDF for you to check. This young man, my brother, was like any other child who grew up in our neighborhood. He was your neighbor's kid who asked to borrow AA batteries for his toy metal detector or sold you raffle tickets for the soccer team. He was your neighbor's kid riding bikes with friends on the block and whose big sister does gymnastics. He was any of them, he was a boy. That article is how the community chose to answer for him.

I guess I should mention we chose to answer by collecting as many of the papers as we could off doorsteps with the help of some friends and dumped the pile at the reporter's house.

A short, stumpy woman with flyway grey hair was Matt's judge, and when we all had to rise for her arrival, I did not. I just noticed how I could barely see her head over the counter. Matt stood in the center beneath that huge mahogany temple of justice. He wore his nicest blue suit, but his same Vans skate shoes. Up to twenty years in jail faced him for distribution of heroin. They gave him the rundown, the scare factor.

Finally Judge Brinkema said, "I'm going to take a chance on you."

Our family sighed in relief, and the gavel hammed down on only one year in prison.

Matt went from federal prisons in Alexandria to several in West Virginia. My weekends, every single one, were spent watching autumn leaves blur by on highways to visit him almost four hours away each way. I used all this time to plan my first novels.

In Alexandria, Matt wore an orange jumpsuit. We lifted up khaki phones and spoke to him through glass. His mood was never panicked. He was cool and almost bored. One time, he coordinated with Dad to pull a trick on me, and Dad spread playing cards on the little ledge of the window. I was told to pick a card in secret, and Matt would close his eyes and pretend to concentrate, then point to the right one. My mouth hit that filthy linoleum prison floor every time (I'm still not entirely sure how they did it), and this lifted the dumbbells off Matt's expression. He was still being my big brother. No matter how bad it was for him, he went out of his way to make me comfortable. No matter what happened, I loved that I was little sister who could always make him feel like a big brother.

As time progressed, Mom jotted down topic ideas all through the week to think of things to say when he rang home. Matt usually went:

"Yeah. Yeah. Huh. I have to go."

In West Virginia, he wore a tan jumpsuit. The guards had buzzcuts and automatics and middle schools educations; they sent visitors away for wearing the wrong type of shoes. Mom was sickeningly sweet to them, not wanting to risk any chance of being denied entry.

A large mural was painted over the security booths. It read: "Integrity Matters." I remember staring at the mural as Dad took off my shoes for the security scanner.

Inside the visiting area, no glass separated us. We claimed a little table and chairs and watched the door for Matt to emerge. When he did, my heart lifted. Mom clapped.

He waddled to us in his baggy jumpsuit and then all I heard were thumps as we took turns hugging him as hard as we could. Mom rocked him side to side, and for me, I could only wait for his arm to circle me.

"Hey, Birdie," he said.

Finding things to talk about was just as hard in person. Mom critiqued his new sleeve of tattoos. Dad inquired about the name the other inmates were calling him as they passed by to meet their own families. "Screech."

I nudged my Converse shoe against Matt's leg, bored.

Matt turned to me. He grinned, and his eyes sparkled as always. "What?"

"Hungry," I said.

"Split some Cheetos?"

He sent me to the vending machine with a few bucks from Dad. Back and forth I went. The crazy thing was that the prison sold baseball hats and postcards too. What the hell would you write on a postcard? *Wish you were here?*

Time was wasted, Matt's growth intellectually and physically shunted, and experiences he did not share—tangles with frightening prison social structures he'd never imagined—hardened and hurt him. He did read, and he took classes which allowed him to earn his GED inside the walls of the jail, but I can't imagine how academic that really was. That graduation reminded me of my own. Both Matt and I had flung our caps ironically—me because mine flopped perhaps an inch off my knee and onto the floor with my dystrophic weakness, and Matt because the other inmates pulled their brows together in irony as only he threw it to the ceiling. On each occasion, we'd both laughed and looked at our parents.

The last prison I'll describe that Matt stayed at briefly was called Warsaw. It was a no-human-contact facility. They slipped his meals under the door. Urine and feces would sometimes be left in the hall.

Prison was not Matt.

But sometimes I think prison helped make him.

Years later, when Matt had been released for some time, he slept in the pullout bed beneath mine. Dad, my usual caretaker, was gone on business. Usually I'd want Mom to substitute. She turned me best and knew all my nooks and muscles. For some reason, though, I asked Matt instead.

Years ago we would have been here drawing our dwarves and elves on the bed. Lately we drew different ideas in our heads when we spoke. Sometimes it was still fantasy, especially if a new video game came out we wanted to discuss. I'd gotten almost as good as he was now. Almost. When we played *Halo,* he still had to let me hide in corners to respawn my energy shields while plasma bullets spouted from his gun. But when I got angry with him—when he stole something or yelled—I played alone, wandering lost for hours on a stupid map of some stupid game, and he's sit there on the couch watching, knowing I was angry at him, neither of us speaking. Finally, he'd say, "You have to unlock the sword in the Academy before you can go there." So I'd unlock the sword in the Academy and solve all my video game-ish problems. I'd smile. We'd talk again.

Other sleepovers as of late might look like me holding his hand and listening. Listening. Sometimes speaking. Sometimes, when I didn't know what to say to help, I told him stories. It's all I know how to do. But I rubbed my thumb on his knuckle with every word. I remember him listening to one in particular: a legend I once heard about a good wolf and a bad wolf fighting in every person. "Do you know which one wins?" I said.

"The bad wolf," said Matt, his eyes still closed.

"The one you feed," I whispered.

He didn't reply, hand still in mine, and that's how I knew I took away some of his aloneness. Isn't that why I wanted to write?

I'm not haunted that Matt hurt. We all do. I'm haunted to think he might ever have hurt alone.

I don't know that I was ever as conflicted inside as Matt thought my disease made me, but I struggled just enough that when he spiraled into his own illness, he felt we could suffer together. I was a decent companion. But sometimes I wish it hurt more so I could have been a better one.

My eyes were closed now. I tried to sleep.

"Shea?" said Matt.

"Yeah?"

I heard him rustle on the pillow. "I like sleeping next to you."

"Why?" I said. "I make you flip me like five times a night."

"I don't care. It gives me purpose."

"You have a lot of purpose besides me."

"No, I don't."

I paused. I could try to convince him otherwise. But with five novels under my belt now, I felt I had the vocabulary I needed to make him feel understood.

"You feel isolated from the world, don't you, Matt?"

More silence. Facing the wall, I could only picture his expression.

"How did you know?" he said.

"Because," I said. "I saw you through the glass in prison." My voice was low. "It feels like the glass isn't gone, doesn't it?"

He didn't answer. He didn't speak for some time. I thought I offended him.

And when his reply finally came, it was full of tears.

"It never left."

SIX

NOVEMBER 2017

A Facebook Messenger icon popped onto my screen. I sighed, but opened it right away.

WILL: hey

SHEA: Hey bud.

There was a pause. My eyes hung on the phone. The young man messaging me had tattoos like Matt did; gauges in his ears. They used to spend hours on our couch playing video games. Matt was sad when he moved to Michigan.

WILL: how u holding up?

SHEA: Thanks for checking <3 It's

different each day. I'm in therapy. Coping with flashbacks and stuff.

I made to return to the eBay auction I was trying to snipe, but Will shot messages back faster than I could switch tabs.

WILL: couple days ago I was thinking about matt was a hard day. I deal with a lot of guilt for leaving. Two weeks after I left he was gone. really fucked me up

SHEA: I get you. But I think it had nothing to do with that. It was just coincidence.

WILL: I'm sorry I wasn't there for him. I feel like maybe if I didn't leave he'd still be here

SHEA: You know nothing and no one could have stopped him

WILL: i just wish there was something I could of done. I talked to him that night.

SHEA: It's not your fault.

I pictured Robin Williams from *Good Will Hunting* in

my head.

WILL: i'm sorry if u don't feel like talking about this i just don't know who else to talk to about it

I paused. My body was rigid, my breathing tight. He was right; I didn't want to talk about this. But Will was in pain. I couldn't leave him.

SHEA: You can always talk to me. I'm right here for you, day and night. It wasn't your fault. He used when he was happy and sad and angry and relaxed and hopeful and depressed.

WILL: i felt like he was my brother. we became so close. neither of us expected this to happen

SHEA: None of us did. And it wasn't your fault. He wasn't counting on you. You were buddies. That's all there is to it. Everyone needs buddies.

WILL: but i trusted matt with my life

SHEA: I know you loved him. He loved you too.

WILL: yeah

There was a pause. I glanced at the other things happening on Facebook: someone's dog in a Halloween Superman cloak. A copy-paste post asking friends to comment in one sentence how they met you.

WILL: it's always the good ones i swear

I didn't need time to think of my response.

SHEA: You're a good one and you're still here.

WILL: ive been clean now for a month might not seem like much but for me its a lot

SHEA: Not a lot? That's amazing. I'm so proud of you. That doesn't make you any less deserving of happiness.

WILL: im not sure what i deserve to be honest with u

SHEA: You have a heartbeat and a purpose. So you deserve respect and happiness.

WILL: Wow. Thank you. I'm really happy that ive been able to talk to u and ur mom about everything i really appreciate it I was expecting you guys to tell me to fuck off i wont lie. i was sick too you know

SHEA: I would never want that. I hope
you will always stay in my life.

WILL: i would like that

Sometime after, I fell asleep. I was woken too early
the next day for work, the tips of my fingers cold. Light
speared my eyes and I groaned.

Mom pulled a brush through my hair and tugged on a
slim plaid button-down. She didn't talk much.

"Something wrong?" I said.

"It's okay," said Mom. "It's just a call I got this
morning."

"What do you mean?" I said.

"I don't know if you remember Matt's friend Will."

I froze.

"He OD'ed last night."

Someone knocked on the back door, and I jumped at the
kitchen island. Mom screamed with delight and raced
for the handle.

Matt stood there, grinning. Knowing he had surprised
us. Mom ripped the door open. "You loser!" she jested,
and then hugged him hard. Tears already in her eyes.
They laughed.

Dad walked up the steps to the back door next, in his

brown suede coat. He smiled.

Matt was home from prison, just in time for the holidays.

The next few months ushered in an exhausting cycle of federal, rehabilitative probation. He didn't get a little security band around his ankle, but he may as well have gotten one attaching him to Mom. The program forbade him to drive but also required him to attend appointments, therapy, Narcotics Anonymous. Mom drove him on top of driving me everywhere.

Matt and I didn't talk much. I was running out of things to say. But we clung to our relationship over the Xbox. About halfway through the campaign of *Gears of War 2*, split screen, I loosened up. Our joysticks and buttons clacked around and I laughed with him when I died (if he didn't get mad) and felt pride stretch my chest when I rescued him from his knees and dove away fast, revving my chainsaw.

In the middle of taking down the Locust Queen, there was a knock at the front door and the dogs rushed for it, their nails clicking a crescendo on the hardwood floors. They *woofed!* loud and fast.

The probation officer walked in, clipboard under his arm. He was bald, tan-skinned, with a lazy eye and a wobbling walk. Ironically he always grinned and laughed. Mom liked him. He was sort of that one teacher in juvenile detention that still treated you like a human.

Matt paused the game. I waited with the controller on my knee. Randomly the officer would arrive to drug test Matt and check up.

For the entire year of probation—to the best of my knowledge, anyway—Matt was clean.

They had a little ceremony for him when he completed the year and they reinstated his freedom to him. It was in the courtroom with the same squat, grey-haired female judge, Brikema. Matt had asked if I would give the speech before the jury witnessing this legal proceeding.

So, with nerves vibrating my body and a handful of index cards under my seatbelt, I approached the table and microphone. All eyes set upon me—cop, jury, judge, and lawyer. I looked at Judge Brinkema first. And then I spoke.

I remember every word of my speech. But only one part needs to be recounted.

I said to Matt, in front of everyone, "You are not a harmer. You're a helper. You're a healer."

I looked him in the eye. He looked at me in his dark blue suit, hands crossed in front of him, eyes red with tears. But smiling at me.

"Heroes bleed, Matt. And through all of this, you are still mine."

A tear dribbled down my cheek too.

The court gifted him an Alcoholics Anonymous book, and everyone signed it, including the judge, with well-wishes. I remember thinking it was weird that they didn't give him a book for Narcotics Anonymous. If only Matt were addicted to alcohol. Yes, alcohol withdrawal can kill you whereas drug withdrawal cannot, but accidental deaths are so much less common in alcohol. Alcohol has so much less stigma.

Things were looking good for Matt. The year got him healthy again. His pallor gone; his face full and bright.

Getting a job remained the most difficult task. With goodwill, many offered Matt what some might call "blue collar" work. Shoveling pavement or cleaning out garages. This is equal and honorable labor, and he did every job with gratitude. But few stopped to ponder whether Matt dreamed of other careers. Every single application, even to low entry positions, asked for criminal records, and every job that excited him denied him. Creating futures for people with addictions—and thus, those oftentimes with brushes with the law—calls on corporate cooperation too. I once suggested to Mom that she campaign for companies of our horizon like Google or Amazon to offer entry level jobs or trainings for individuals with two or more years of sobriety completed.

Even the military refused Matt's attempt to join.

I think about this often. To me, who could be a better

leader than Matt? He got in anyone's face who bullied me. He helped me reach chips on the high shelf. He shared on every social media outlet me singing him a song about overcoming addiction Christmas morning, despite how vulnerable it made him look. Heaven was never further from anyone but him, and still he called me his angel. I wonder who would be a better leader than someone who has seen horrors of humanity so young, who stayed holding the hand of a passed out fellow-addict at a party while everyone else ran, who fought every day for his health, who faced constant rejection, whose many American rights were stripped after prison, and still wanted to serve. When will we realize that the best leaders are the broken ones? Martin Luther King, Jr. attempted suicide in his youth. Abraham Lincoln likely had major depressive disorder. Mental opposition and even illness provide experiences that meet the criteria of resilience, strength, and compassion leaders need. They allow followers to look into the leader's eyes and see they've been there.

I still think about this today. I know Matt is gone. But I guess I'm a little broken too now. If I can lead with a limp, I will.

When I turned eighteen and first voted around the time Matt's probation ended, I puffed up my crooked chest and strutted (as one does on wheels) with my *I*

Voted sticker. It did not dawn on me until later why Matt only glanced at the news channel's election results with somberness as he leaned on the wall in his grey jacket and beanie hat. As a felon, at that present time, his right to vote had been indefinitely taken away, and now as an adult who has never missed an election, I understand what kind of hope and control that robs a person. What intensified this, I'm sure, is how greatly Matt needed the government to aide his journey, and how completely he must have felt that the government made sure not to listen.

I am frustrated with legislation proposals that begin with "Crack down on…" As our family had learned, there was no *fiercer this* or *tighter that* that could remove Matt's addiction and the behaviors it pioneered. No patriarchal figure in a leather armchair could invite Matt into his office, cross his hands on the desk, and have a "hard talk" that straightened out the disease that was chemical. I never knew what the answer was, but I've thought of it in silence while staring at my ballot every time. I know there is right and wrong, I know thousands of factors exist. Looking now, I just want my brother back, and if safe and legal doses of the drug (as they've done in Portugal to address their own opioid crisis) administered in a medical setting to addicted people with little chance of recovery (like Matt) could have kept him with me,

I'd've accompanied Matt to every appointment.

As time went on, Matt never opened that Alcoholics Anonymous book, but I saw him trying. He tried in ways he knew how, and got frustrated as anyone would have. What was most important to all of us, again, was that the probation he had just graduated from had kept him sober for the longest unbroken period he had ever achieved.

But the random drug tests ended.

A week later, Matt relapsed.

A week. Just a week.

We let it go. It was a slip. He confessed. He felt so bad.

Then another relapse. Oops.

Then another.

How many times does one relapse before one is simply considered using again?

The last thing we wanted was for Matt to once more be apprehended. We hushed it up and packaged him away up north, to a beach home in the Hamptons we owned. He's got to get away from his friends and the toxic area, we said.

The only problem was that while Northern Virginia had toxic areas, so did Long Island.

He relapsed there too.

We had no choice but to send him to his fourth rehab.

It was called Seabrook, and it was a four-week program in New Jersey. For a long four days, the family needed to attend a workshop too. A teenager, unable to care for myself alone, I was uncommunicative on the drive up. Frustrated. Taken from all my plans and friends for yet another program.

Here we go again.

Funnily enough, the rehab support circles liked what I said, and I had a lot to say. They encouraged me as I laid into Mom and said she enables Matt by not kicking him out when he lies and steals. They even encouraged me when I laid into Dad who laid into me for laying into Mom. Dad *let* her enable him.

The head counselor was an old man with a gravelly Jersey accent but eyes deep with compassion. He would sit at the head of the circle, legs crossed, and nod and nod and nod. I don't think I saw him write on his clipboard once.

Finally, our loved ones in treatment were welcome to join the workshop with us. Families sprang up and hugged them, but I remember thinking what rookies they were. I was almost over the whole tearful reunion thing.

Then Matt walked right into my periphery on my left. My heart fluttered.

I guess I wasn't over it.

We realized something was wrong when the other patients announced to cheers that they had agreed twenty-eight days was not enough to cement their sobriety, and they had chosen to continue rehab. Matt did not.

We were broken up into private groups to talk as a family. I could hear the chatter of other families.

Our little room was quiet. Matt, while not cantankerous, had nothing to say. His arms were crossed. Mom began to cry. Dad's jaw shifted side to side.

I stole this little squishy stress ball from the shelf and played with it.

On my way to the water fountain, I caught the head counselor.

"Why is Matt not better?" I said. "His head isn't any better."

The counselor looked at me with a sympathetic frown as if this wasn't news to him.

"If he doesn't want to yet, he's just not going to be ready to change."

But of course Matt wants to change, I thought. It's just that the wrong wolf is hungrier.

We loaded the car with few words. It was overcast, chilly. New patients watched us as they smoked cigarettes under a tree.

Mom handed over my wallet and told me to go buy any snacks I wanted from the convenience shop in the rehab lobby.

I went inside to the cramped store. I grabbed gum,

chips, and a sweet tea. The register counter was as high as a bank teller's.

While the clerk rang me up, I noticed a box of coins behind her. Shiny bronze, green, purple, blue, red, and silver, like Mardi Gras beads. I asked to see them.

They were sobriety tokens. One for two years, five years, ten years, twenty years, thirty years, and fifty years. $5 each. All together in my hand, they weighed almost a pound. I imagined that fifty-year coin waiting in my jewelry box for so long, and one day, Matt and I both white-haired and old, having only each other left, giving it to him.

I bought every single coin.

I never could have known that all six would stay in my box forever.

SEVEN

DECEMBER 2017

"There's Matt," said Mom. "He comes to visit me every day." She looked out her home office window. I followed her gaze. A red cardinal played in the bird bath in the shrubs.

Mom believed Matt was the cardinal after a few spiritual experiences. Dad believed. Kelley believed.

I said the cardinal was the state bird of Virginia. Because, you know. There's a lot of them.

Nevertheless, I bought her a glass cardinal suncatcher that day and left it on her desk with no note to find the next morning.

A few weeks later was the full moon. We banged closed car doors from errands and scaled the hill up the driveway. Mom looked at the moon.

"There's my baby," she said.

I tried to muffle my sigh. But I couldn't keep the slight annoyance from my voice. "He's the moon now, too?"

"He's everywhere to me," she said.

So why is he nowhere to me?

JANUARY 2015

"Max, move," I said.

Our russet-gold, 100lb Lab looked up at me with doleful eyes and pushed-back ears. Heat coursed through me though, and I had no patience for him being in my way tonight.

"Come on, Max."

Max pushed himself off the floor, hind legs shaking, and stumped off to the other side of the room. It seemed like yesterday Dad had lifted him from the cardboard box like Rafiki on Pride Rock and placed him into Matt's lap Christmas Day. The little ball of fuzz sat there in Matt's arms and jolted with "hiccy-pups." That was nearly eight years ago.

"Sorry, Max," said Mom behind me, but my way to the sitting room was finally clear. I veered into my parking spot at the arm of the couch and waited. Arms crossed.

Mom lowered onto the couch, and then Matt followed, sitting on the other one. He looked way too relaxed;

muscles too loose, easy smile. He even leaned forward and tried to beckon Max over with his hand.

"Okay, Shea, you first," said Mom.

Family meeting. I let them have it.

"I should be allowed to choose when I go to the bathroom," I said.

There. Some fucking thesis statement.

Max's tail thumped the floor and he finally rose and waddled over to Matt. Matt's grin widened.

"It's not fair to have someone decide for me," I went on, "and it's pretty degrading. Do you want me to decide for you when you shower?"

"Honey," said Mom, "you need to realize that more than one person goes into making that happen for you."

"Trust me, I'm aware."

"And now that Daddy's working in New York for a little, you need to be more cooperative to Matt's time. I can't lift you myself like he can."

Max opened his mouth and rubbed up against Matt, who patted his stomach hard.

"Matt has a right to ask for you to be ready to go to the bathroom at a certain time. He wants to plan his evenings too and be free to see friends and go out."

"So I can't control my own body, then?" My voice was getting louder. "I can't choose when to go to the bathroom. How is that okay?"

"I can't believe you're being so unreasonable," said Mom.

"Me?! I'm being unreasonable?! You're telling me that I don't get to decide my own bodily functions. You get to go to the bathroom whenever you feel like it; I have to schedule a damn appointment and give my insurance card. How is that—?"

"You know what?" Mom and I looked over to a new voice. Matt's. He was lying back on the couch, one hand contemplatively at his chin. His tone was genuine. "She's right."

My eyebrows rose. I stared at him. "I am?"

Matt swung forward and stood. "Yes," he said. "I wouldn't want to be told that either. No more schedule."

He moved up and tickled my shoulder, walking right past me.

My face flushed with color.

I've been told by everyone who really knew him that there was nothing Matt loved more than me. I believed it. I also believed that he could play everyone else like a whistle but me. So when he went to Calabasas, California for his sixth rehab about half a year later, I took the weekly family phone calls with his counselor with a chunk of salt. As usual, the counsellor reported that Matt blamed some of his suffering on me and my disease, just like he did at the wilderness camp. I raised an eyebrow, put the phone on speaker, and munched on some pretzels.

While I doubted Matt was truly opening up to his therapist, there was no avoiding the fact that his body was healing. Two weeks off heroin turns to two months off heroin and the next thing I know, I'm visiting Matt with the Hollywood hills behind him. Young men and women waving at him with smiles. Sun in his hair. He had a navy blue sport coat on, pink shirt unbuttoned at the collar, and sleeves hanging loose without cuffs. Skateboard under his arm, Matt gave us the tour of the halfway house neighborhood he lived in. A halfway house is a little apartment a bunch of recovering addicts live in together to keep each other accountable to sobriety, and it's the first transition phase out from in-patient rehab. Matt always preferred the halfway house phase, whereas I always felt he was never halfway ready for it.

But he looked happy.

Oh, how we wanted him happy.

It made him unhappy when Mom woke to a police car in front of our house and a new warrant for his arrest hammered at the door. It was for a crime he committed long before California. The offense was not violent; it was not even distribution. It was possession in his car. Our family begged the court to let him stay in Calabasas, and explained that this was finally getting him sober. The rehab was willing to keep him for a whole year—exactly what he needed, and what the other places didn't offer.

The Commonwealth of Virginia refused, and Matt was required to leave his halfway house, his progress, and his sober support system in sunny California and return home to play by probation's rules.

Matt's butt found the couch again, his phone buzzed with old contacts, and it was bad news.

Several nights he cried with all of us surrounding him, not knowing what to do. The only option we had was to wait it out. To get through probation—thank God it wasn't another prison sentence—and get back to California the hour after it's through. Matt grieved for his freedom. And one night, while I was scrolling my phone in the metal bleachers of my friend's high school field hockey game, I saw a photo of a big, black Honda Shadow motorcycle on Matt's Facebook page. I cursed.

Did Mom and Dad really just buy him that? I thought that was going to be his incentive to work and save?

But he was happy.

Oh, how we wanted him happy.

Life went on through probation, and Matt's bike roared in and out of the garage for mandatory counseling appointments and drug tests. California seemed a distant memory.

Another new addition to this deal was a prescribed

drug called Suboxone, intended to reduce the urge for opiates. It's been circulated since 1981, but has some nasty catches. It's addictive in and of itself, makes you violently ill without it, and triggers even more depression. Still it was better than heroin. Heroin could kill you. Suboxone couldn't. Matt used it as needed, but because Suboxone sold for $40 a pop on the street, Mom and Dad hid our supply. Two Suboxone pills could be sold for one hit of heroin.

It's important to understand this in order to understand the events that happened next.

On a night like any other, I sat in front of the flat screen playing my favorite video game. A fight brewed in my periphery. Matt wanted to go to a "friend's" house. At midnight. And he needed $100. For "a bet" he owed. Or else.

Uh huh.

I kept playing my video game, eyes hooked to the screen, as Mom stomped downstairs and told Matt to sit down and Matt said no and started raiding the drawers for change and Dad paced and shook his head and Mom demanded Dad do something and Matt said we were all "fucking insane." I bought a new sword at the blacksmith and fast-traveled to the nearest Mages Guild for my next quest.

"I swear, Mom, I can't tell you what it's for, but it's not

for drugs," said Matt.

"We all know that's a lie, Matt," I said, casting a fire spell at the troll, which obviously shows I was a little distracted because trolls are immune to fire.

"Shut up, Shea," said Matt.

"Just stop lying," I said.

"Honey, please, this is not smart," said Mom. "Please don't go."

"I have to, Mom. I promise I'll pay you back. Please. If you don't give me the money, I have to steal from Walmart. I don't want to, Mom, please."

"Seriously, Matt?" I said.

"Shut UP, Shea."

"Matt, you're not going out," said Dad.

"Fuck you," said Matt, "I'm twenty-six years old, you can't tell me what to do."

"You're not going, Matthew," said Mom.

And Matt exploded and stormed up the stairs and started banging around his bedroom.

"What is he doing?" I said, still kinda monotone.

"I don't know," said Dad. "I'm sorry, sweetie."

"Don't apologize to me." I hated when Dad did that.

A few minutes later, Matt skirted down the stairs. "I need Suboxone."

"What?" said Mom. This was ridiculous, so I paused the game and joined them.

"I need Suboxone or I swear I'm gonna use so I don't wake up," said Matt.

"Okay," said Mom. "Larry, do you have any?"

Dad's expression was tight. "I'll look." He disappeared into my first-floor bedroom.

Matt continued to pull his hair and curse. "You MOVED it AGAIN. That is MY prescription!"

"Calm down," said Dad a minute later. And he produced a single wrapper of the pill, like a hand wipe wrapper. With careful fingers, Dad pried it apart. The little pill fell into his palm. "Here."

Matt snatched it like a starved man snatches bread. He hurried towards the front door while Dad and Mom mumbled dark words to each other. And then—

"Oh my God," said Matt. "Oh my God. I dropped it." He pounded back towards us. "I dropped the goddamn pill. I can't find it."

"Calm down," Dad said again. "We'll look on the floor."

"Oh my God," said Matt.

"We'll find it," said Mom.

"Oh my GOD."

I couldn't catch anyone's eye. So I snuck into my room, grabbed a pen and paper, and wrote. While Matt patrolled the hallway to the door looking for the lost pill and Mom shuffled around her purse looking for a second one, I showed the note I scrawled to my parents. It read:

He is pretending to lose the first pill so you'll get him a second one so he can sell both.

Mom and Dad stopped. They exchanged looks. I stared at them with a set, sure expression.

"I found another one," said Matt, now from Mom's office. Mom rushed to him.

"Please, Matt." She was crying now. "Please don't leave."

I followed just after. "Matt, please," I said. "Don't leave."

"I have to," he said.

I sighed. Shook my head. "All right, Matt. Then I'm just going to park in front of the door."

"Please don't," he said.

"I have to." I echoed him.

I moved my 300lb wheelchair in front of the door, pressed its metal into the wood frame, and flipped on the brakes.

Matt stood in front of me. Mom, exhausted, sat in silence in her office.

"Please move, Shea," said Matt.

"Nope."

He reached over and jiggled the doorknob out, but my wheelchair blocked it.

"This is stupid, Shea."

"I'm not moving," I said.

"I'll just use the other door."

"Fine," I said.

And so he did.

He slammed the garage door. A moment later, his Honda Shadow growled. The rumble reverberated into the distance and he was gone.

I stayed at the door and refused to flip off my brakes.

Moisture filled my eyes and I hung my head.

EIGHT

The white circle swung clockwise in the center of the YouTube video. It buffered to black and although my posture was tense and dignified I held my breath.

In a few moments would be the first time I heard my brother's voice in ten months.

Matt adjusted the camera in the video. He laughed, and I flinched. There it was.

His hand found his mouth and he flicked up his eyebrows in a funny way, looking into the lens. Behind him and to the right sat his friend Cullen. Cullen wore glasses and a striped hoodie. On his lap was a super thug looking electronic mixer.

"All right, all right." Matt giggled. "Let's do it."

Cullen looked at the camera and raised his arm with a little downward swish of his hand like they were about to drop the hottest beat.

And then my laptop practically shook as an electronic bass line pulsed on the video. Matt rubbed his hands together and started to rap into the corner of the screen.

I shook my head. A little huff of breath inflated my smile. Sweet rhymes were being sizzled ba'dizzled and random gangsta signs being tossed and Matt spouting lyrics fresher than Whole Foods.

It fizzled into fits of laughter and Matt actually having joy and fun in his life. That happened.

But that's where I always paused.

Happened.

Past tense.

This video is a collection of colored pixels playing.

Just because Matt moved and thought in it does not mean he moved and thought now.

In months past I had not searched for videos of Matt for this reason. Seeing him animated and not frozen in an image I knew would be a jarring experience. Almost a taunting one. "Remember this life form?" the YouTube video would say. "Does it seem like he is here? Feel familiar? HA! He is dead. Now take a Tide ad!"

I had heard since his death, "He is in a better place." "He watches over you." And even from mediums claiming to connect with him, "Matt is in the infant stages of his life review. He was as shocked by his death as you were."

Everyone asserting that he still is conscious.

But I felt the body. I felt the stillness. I heard the screams of my parents.

Matthew Joseph Megale was not conscious.

Even as I write this now, some terror stretches through my stomach. Years ago I gave death an eyebrow wriggle and shouldered by. Ever since March 4, 2017, I became a coward.

Horrified endlessly of the nowhere. For it seemed to me just too far-fetched, too good to be true, too much of exactly what I wanted for Matt to be anywhere but nowhere.

And guess who's going nowhere next?

So I did what any sensible person would do when confronted with a hundred-thousand-year-old life mystery. I made haste for the Internet.

I Googled all the greatest scientific minds of the age and probed their beliefs. Maybe if one of these geniuses believed in the possibility of an afterlife, there was a chance for Matt and me.

Neil deGrasse Tyson looked the nicest, so I gave him a shot. Bzzzt. Strike one. No evidence, he said. Become worm food, he said. Circle of life, he said. Larry King was the interviewer and insisted that he cannot tolerate the idea of eternal nonexistence. It kind of made me feel better that Larry King was with me on this.

Michio Kaku—no.

Stephen Hawking—hell no.

Atheism was like tobacco to me. No matter how long I stayed sober and how many resources I explored to stay off it (agnosticism was like the patch you smack onto your neck) I just couldn't shake it.

"What do you mean by terror?" one of the mediums had said.

"Of death," I said, "for him and for me."

"Do you feel it's near?" Oh shit, is she asking me or telling me?

"No...not necessarily." Pause. "Um. Right?"

"Right," she said. Couldn't she be, like...lying? Mercifully? I swallowed. "You won't be alone," she went on.

Yes, I am good at filling my life with people to love and who love me. I guess I wasn't surprised. And thankfully I had once met a palm reader who said I have a long life line so if this medium was being coy then they can just throw crystals at each other to the death to resolve who is right.

It wasn't until later that I questioned my interpretation of her words: "You won't be alone."

Maybe she didn't mean my bedside wouldn't be empty of my future children and friends and many lovers.

Maybe she meant I'd see Matt before.

And suddenly that's the only thing I grasped onto. I willed myself to believe this somehow.

Matt will come to me before it happens.

And if he doesn't come, it won't happen.

I clung to this to shield me from the terror.

But part of me still can't help but wonder and grieve at one question.

Who came to him?

JANUARY 2017

I don't mean to brag or anything, but I kinda ran the show at The Writers of Chantilly.

They're groaning and rolling their eyes reading this now. Hi, everyone.

Come on, though. They know I burst into the doors with a bang and slap down my chapters like they're warrants to hand over compliments lest I send the librarians in to push them onto the table with handcuffs and read them their rights.

My writing group met a few Mondays a month to share stories and encourage one another. Sometimes to destroy things, too, I guess. In reality, the table had become family to me. Our Chieftain sat on my right and directed the reader list. She wore glasses and had reddish brown hair and I noticed my business card from four years ago still stapled to the inside of her folder. There was Tom, the adventure writer with a deep voice that would melt any woman's anything. Robert's writing smelled of salt, sweat, and fear as he wrote about sharks. There was Angela and Pat and Brian and John. Nick knows I blubber and gush when talking about him and we both get all red and wave bashful hands at each other.

If I did not mention the other members, it is because they were not there the night I got the text from my brother.

MATT: I'm sorry I'm such a screw up. I just need to be homeless for a while and live on the streets. I'll see you when I get my life together.

My heart pounded. In the middle of Brian's chapter on the Knights Templar, I texted Dad.

SHEA: What happened? What is going on?

Brian's words hit and fell off my ears as I waited for the reply. It came in, and I learned.

Matt was in the police station in Baltimore after being released from the hospital. He had taken my handicapped van when Mom and Dad were away, driven it to Baltimore to buy drugs, took them, passed out behind the wheel, and crashed the car.

"Excuse me." I pulled my wheelchair away from

the writer's table. Everyone looked up. I turned to the Chieftain. "Could you get the door please?"

Brian went on as I tried to "slip" out, but wheels clunked into walls and my motor clicked. John's eyes darted up to me while trying to concentrate on the page. Shea leaving a writer's meeting was unheard of.

Somehow I turned over the rubber grooves of my wheels enough to reach the PBS DVD rental area of the library where no one ever was.

I sat there and stared into nothing and shook.

Matt almost died tonight. This was the extreme of opioid addiction. He'd lost friends to it, both socially and to overdose, and still he went. He had to steal the car and drive two hours north, and still he went. Baltimore or Richmond were Northern Virginia's import hubs, and Matt's phone was clogged with filth luring him up.

He did that all for one hit. Just one. Just a few hours of high.

But it's more than that. It's more than high. It's also an absence of illness. Withdrawal from heroin, while it cannot kill you the way alcohol withdrawal can, punished the body. Flu, stomach virus, and broken ribs all at once. I remembered one of Matt's friend's saying to us, "I don't think he wants the high anymore, I think he wants to just not be sick."

Couldn't he see it made him sick so much worse than physically?

Thoughts exploded like artillery in my head. Dad said he was on his way to drive to Baltimore and back to pick Matt up. He would send our dear family friends to come get me—they'd roll up in our clunky green Ford with a metal lift that screeched like a banshee we used for emergencies. Matt almost died. Matt almost died. Matt almost died.

A Facebook message popped in my phone. It was John from the writer's table.

JOHN: You okay?

I thought about it for a second. I rocked a little in my chair because suddenly I felt sick too.

SHEA: Can you come out?

Nearly that second the door clicked open a few yards away and John cut to me faster than I'd ever seen him do. His blue eyes were deep with worry, expecting the worst, and he did not pause to approach me.

"My brother overdosed," I said, voice shaky, keeping it together. "He survived, but he—"

John didn't let me finish. He dove to me and pulled me into him. I let go and sobbed into his large chest. My hand ripped into his forearm and waves of tremors showered through me.

You never believe it will be you. Your family. Your brother. Part of me still chose to believe it couldn't get worse than this. But it could.

Two months later, John would be holding me the same exact way.

This time, behind him, would be a table of flowers and a slideshow of Matt.

And I wished, for once, that the end could just be another story on the writing group table.

They could destroy that one all they want.

Please, I thought. *Destroy it.*

NINE

The weird thing was I never ate salad. Of all the food in the world, choosing salad to me was like choosing to give up on life. I asked for salad that night. It was Matt's salad, the only healthy food he ate and would promptly wash down with four cans of Coca-Cola. Dad, unknowing of its spoken-for status, served me the store-bought salad and poured raspberry lemonade.

It was around 10:00 p.m. I figured I'd take the heat from Matt later.

The following is an account of the events of the night we found Matt dead. Times are approximate. This cannot be a narrative.

I'd say reader discretion advised, but I do not think I can bear to be alone with this page.

22:00   I crunch the salad as I watch *Everybody Loves Raymond.* Piano music is stuck in my head.

22:05   I ask for a refill of my lemonade.

22:10   Dad knocks on the bathroom door in the living room and calls Matt's name. The door is locked and the yellow light inside glows through the doorframe.

22:11   He knocks and calls his name again. I stop chewing.

22:12   Dad storms into the kitchen, jacks open a drawer, and rummages in it for a tool—plyers, bottle opener, anything. I pause the TV and ask if I should call 911. I already know something is very wrong.

22:13   I race past Dad as he curses and slams the drawer shut, finding no effective tool. My wheel hits the base of the staircase on the other side of the house and I shout to wake

Mom. I yell to her, "Is Matt in his room?" She scrambles to his room and calls down no.

22:14   Mom takes three stairs at a time. I follow her to the bathroom door where Dad is yanking the handle and shaking the doorframe. Still calling Matt's name.

22:15   Mom follows Dad into the laundry room. He reappears with a screwdriver. He pries in the screwdriver and jiggles the lock three or four times. I poise my cell phone in my hand; the dial screen is up. Mom is right behind him.

22:16   Just as Dad breaks the lock, I dive away so I can't see what they'd find. Somehow I know. Mom and Dad scream his name. Mom shouts, "Oh my God, he's BLUE!" They cry for me to call 911.

22:17   I barrel into Mom's home office and speak to the 911 operator. "My brother overdosed, please send help." Dad carries Matt to the couch and begins mouth-to-mouth resuscitation, pounds his chest, but I don't see any of this. I hear it all. I can't leave the room and look. I glance at

Mom's sewing machine and fabric baskets as this all happens. Max, our dog, runs to where Mom and Dad and Matt are. He barks and barks and barks. He is braver than me.

22:18   "Is he breathing?" the operator asks. I relay the question. "No!" my parents shout. Dad yells, "God, please!" Mom yells, "Matt!" Dad yells, "Don't take him!"

22:19   Max barks and barks and barks.

22:20   The operator, a calm woman, tells me she needs to walk us through CPR. Mom's heavy footsteps thump to me in a sprint as she reaches for the phone. She is still in her pajamas.

22:21   Mom and Dad take turns doing CPR and pounding his chest. Mom tells me to go outside and flag down the ambulance.

22:22   I sled down the driveway and into the street. It is a cold night. I see my breath. I look at the stars. I chant, "Please bring Matt back, please bring Matt back." They look back at me helpless.

22:24   Ambulance sirens.

22:25   A firetruck and ambulance park in front of my
          house. They are so slow. Why do they not run?

22:26   "Please help," I chirp with both terror and
          cold at two EMTs. Somehow I make them
          slower because they stop and turn to me and
          watch me for a long beat in the flashing red
          lights. I realize they thought I was asking
          them to help *me*. Eventually they go inside.

22:30   Footsteps, people in our house. Max barks and
          barks and barks.

22:31   Mom and Dad come to where I am huddled
          in fear in another room. Still I have not seen
          Matt. They drape their arms on me and say
          the Lord's Prayer over and over and over. I join
          them, but it is the last time to date I will ever
          repeat this prayer.

22:35   I close my eyes as a stretcher bumps over out
          front door threshold.

22:45   We follow the ambulance to Fairfax Hospital,

but it outraces us. Something has snapped in me. I repeat aloud, "It's okay, it's okay, it's okay." I belong in a straitjacket.

23:15   We are in the waiting room. Mom and Dad sit together on a bench. Eyes puffy and full of tears. They look at each other. I will never forget how they look at each other.

23:35   A young brunette nurse comes out. She asks us to follow her into the back. Her voice is disgustingly pleasant and placating. The room is titled "Family Consultation Room." It is over.

23:36   Mom wants it straight. MOM: "Did he make it?" NURSE: "No, he didn't." Her voice was like the way a teacher tells a first grader the class goldfish died.

23:37   We all break down.

23:44   The doctor comes in. He is Indian. He sits. I like his voice better. "We tried for 40 minutes. We got one heartbeat."

00:10   We are led to the body. I close my eyes and

move my chair into the room blind. Dad kisses him. Mom kisses him. Then they both lift me into their arms and heave me over the table so I can kiss him too. My hand is smushed into his fingers. They are long and cool, the way that is familiar. "There he is," Mom coos to me. Her voice is sweet. Then I kiss his hair. I whisper something to him. My eyes are always closed.

00:24   There is one final moment where I can turn to see his body one last time. I stop. I do not turn around.

00:28   The hospital asks for our insurance. Money. Money.

00:45   Back in the Consultation Room. I am wailing. Dad pulls me onto his lap on the couch and rocks me.

00:50   The detective comes in. He is short, Hispanic. He wears a police jacket. His expression is sad. His voice is compassionate. "There was a bad batch," he said. "Matt is the eleventh person to die today." We learn that a batch of Fentanyl has circled the area. The youngest victim was twenty-one. The oldest in his fifties.

01:10   We are just sitting. We have not left. We stare. We stare. We stare.

01:20   We call my uncle, wake him in his bed. He must collect my sister in person, since they both live in New York, and she will need arms to fall into. He says, "Fuck. What? Fuck. Oh my God."

01:25   Dad says he wishes he could start this day over again. Mom says, "Our only son." I say nothing. I stare. Piano music plays in my head.

MARCH 4, 2018

A cold wipe ran down my inner forearm. I held it out, upright. The needle approached me.

I tensed, ready for it to penetrate.

Then a rubber-gloved hand lay on my skin. Finn looked up at me.

"Ready?"

"Ready," I said.

"I'm going to do one nice clean line for you first." He pressed a pedal with his foot. The tattoo gun buzzed. "Here we go."

Finn bowed over me. This time, I didn't look away from what I was afraid of.

One straight line of black ink seared into me.

My whole family, Kelley, Mom, and Dad, were behind me, awaiting their turn. It seems now that I am missing a syllable when I list them. That syllable had been gone for one year on this day.

Some of the changes were strange at first. Like how there was no more privacy of thought in the family. When one is quiet, you know where they are, and leave them to it politely. It takes longer now to get from one end of the house to the other. One must pause at photos of him. Or maybe the urn.

In me I noticed even weirder changes. My intolerance for laughter, and anger at ritual for one. Matt never went to church. Why is he ending up in one now? I envied, absurdly, the chaos of gunfire and demand to leave comrades behind without ceremony. And in my lack of feeling, I viewed my tragedy—my intimate, personal tragedy—through the expressions of everyone who hugged my parents when my parents' backs were turned to me. Some closed their eyes in sadness that's too wise, like Grandpa Ed. Others' eyes were wide and speechless, like Uncle Troy's. But no one can say the right thing. I am mad if they mention Matt, and mad if they don't.

You don't get to make him your guiding light; the Uncle Ben to your Spiderman. He was Spiderman.

Other oddities are unwelcome fears. If someone in the house does not answer when you call their name twice, panic sets in, and you beckon louder and more desperately until a door is closed and you hear the laundry machine clunking and know they were only behind the other wall. I no longer could sleep without some human voice on a YouTube video teaching me to carve soap or fix a pair of binoculars, just to fill the suffocating vacuum of the bedsheets.

Once, I saw Max barking at something in the backyard, and convinced myself Mom was laying dead in the grass out of my sight. I waited, and waited, for her to appear, and then stormed out the front door and flagged down a neighbor at his mailbox to race with me to the backyard only to find Mom chatting casually with an old friend. The shed had blocked her from my view from the house, and Max barked at the tennis ball she wasn't throwing. The four of us had stared at each other, dumbfounded. I was mortified.

I had to practice recognizing acts of love again. There seemed no place to begin. "Are my best times in life behind me now?" I'd asked Dad. "Because Matt won't be in anything ahead?" Could there be acts of love without him? So for some reason, in my memory, I tried to focus on the gowns and blazers people wore wore to the funeral. How they'd all stood in their bedrooms, looked in mirrors, to pull on formal clothes for us. That became the first act of love I was able to accept.

The little acts grew. With hesitance, I remembered there were tadpoles wriggling into mud. Food slipping off skillets for me to taste somewhere out there. There were degrees to earn and pretty things to buy and people to love. I am haunted by many things, but I tried to let the electricity of the earth zap life into *my* lump of flesh that used to be a heart, and those distractions were just enough to focus me. They were enough to keep me awake until I could finally sleep.

A year ago. That all was a year ago.

In other circumstances this tattoo parlor, naked tatted women in frames on the wall and shelves of ink in cabinets, was the last place any of us would be. Maybe I'm partly to blame—it was I who chose Finn and I who bought Matt his first tattoo kit one Christmas when he said he'd wanted to be a tattoo artist. He'd used himself as his first canvas, etching in the Italian flag for our 25% Italian blood and a handicapped symbol for me.

Mom had said if he got one more of those nasty things, it'd better be "MOM" across his forehead.

The pain dragged across my flesh. My face did not change. "You sure you haven't done this before?" Finn smirked. He was young with gauges in his ears and tattooed upper arms.

The rest of the family crowded in to watch me. "It's not bad, is it Shea?" Kelley said, surprised by my poise. Her kind, pretty eyes sparkled and her hair fell with beautiful highlights despite being holed up in a bus for fourteen hours to get here for this.

It was bad. But when I compared it to the pain of this past year, not a single muscle twitched. Incubus' *Drive* played on Finn's Pandora as he began the second half of my tattoo.

Would you choose water over wine?

One by one we took the chair and the needle. Each permanently engraving a memorial of Matt into us. Even Mom.

I perched in front of Kelley as she nervous-laughed

and winced at the same time. The needle buzzed over her. "You made this look like it wouldn't hurt," she said. "You're a good pretender."

I just looked at her with love for a long beat.

You have no idea.

As this book now ends, there is one last thing I need to do.

Matt. Listen to me.

Break through hell. Tear down heaven. Destroy the nothing.

Listen to me.

I wanted to go down with your ship. I want your demons.

I want you to haunt me.

Too often I dream of going down your same path. To feel what you felt. I will change my destiny to become a part of yours again.

Fight. Fight to come back to me. Fight to save me again.

Heroes bleed.

I need mine.

That night you overdosed, I suddenly knew exactly what I will see when I die. If there is a there, the first thing I will see is a locked white door.

Light pouring through the cracks.

Somehow I'd glide to it. Closer. Closer.

Except this time, when I opened it...

You. You wouldn't be on the floor. You would be standing there.

Like me.

That night after our tattoos, after all had gone to bed and the house was empty and alone with me, I moved to that bathroom door.

I grabbed the cold handle. I dropped my head and closed my eyes.

I saw the door with the light pouring from the cracks.

My hand turned the knob.

Artwork by
DANNY MUHR

ACKNOWLEDGEMENTS

Thank you to everyone who "gets it."

To the family members who contributed special assistance to the creation of this book: Uncle Roger and Aunt Tiffany Megale, Jack Megale, Maura Fletcher, Will Fletcher, Katie O'Shea, Ryan Kloss.

A very special thank you to everyone who selflessly and generously donated to our GoFundMe page, which is the reason this publication is in your hands today. You answered the call with #IUnderstand.

Thank you to those who were kind to Matt, especially Tom Ghobashi and his family.

Thank you to the friends who surprised me at the wake or funeral: Fellow Lion Jay Moughon, Danny Nash, Michelle Dunlevy, Emma and Mr. Boyd, and Rox Trujillo including. That took courage.

Thank you to Dr. Lorne Ladner. I love and honor you.

To Brother Aaron Goss. To the Church of Jesus Christ of Latter-Day Saints.

Thank you, Danny Muhr, for your beautiful and evocative illustration before these acknowledgments.

Thank you to Bluebullseye Press for making this finished product possible. Thank you to the Writers of Chantilly, especially Barbara Osgood, Terry Williams, Rebecca Thompson, and everyone who came out and waited in that intimidating line, and thank you to the Hourlings for their copyediting and gale of love that took me off my feet—which is, technically, hard to do.

Thank you to my sweet Mike Lannes for the patience and comfort you've lent. To Carol Jones, who remains the brave woman of love I hope to be more like. Thank you Jen Pottheiser, Wes Fleming, Todd Pangman, Jamie Peugh, Chris Caldwell, Polly Herpy, the Nieves family.

Thank you to all who work in addiction treatment, and for especially compassionate justice system employees, who remember in their work people like Matt and people like me. I may not remember your names, I may have only seen your hands or shirt buttons or ID tags in my lowered height and troubled remoteness, but I remember your presence and things you've said.

Thank you to the friends of my parents and sister who support them and unknowingly lift some of the weight from me too—Tony Savarese, George Costas, Sonny Esposito, Maddy Curry, Paige Harrison, Bob Biagi, Nanette Di Falco, Kelly Eisele, and many others. You're my dear friends too.

Thank you to all who I've forgotten in my haze of unreality and human imperfection, who know they were there for us, and who I hope know I love them.

Thank you, personally, to my family: Mom, Dad, Kelley, and Pierre II.

Finally, to our beloved dog Max. You, who will never understand my words, single-handedly kept our family together. I love you, Max. Good boy.

SCM

Carrie Wilken's PhD, the Co-Founder and Clinical Director of The Center for Motivation and Change, is an expert on addiction. This proved to be such a difficult task considering she and Matt never met and he was never her patient, but we are confidant her recommendations will help other families navigate you through the pain of addiction.

-Megan Megale

AFTERWORD

CARRIE WILKENS, PH.D
CO-FOUNDER OF THE CENTER FOR
MOTIVATION AND CHANGE

INTRODUCTION

As a clinician reading this book, I find myself thinking of the countless families I have spoken with who have experienced some version of Shea's story. Family members (and friends) who have loved someone like Matt, someone full of promise, talents, and charms, who also struggled with their use of substances and, in that struggle, caused themselves and the people who love them great pain. And, in all too many cases, lost their life to that struggle.

Loving someone who has a problem with drugs or alcohol can be a journey full of emotional highs and lows, moments of complete confusion and despair, as well precious moments of hope and healing. With the explosion of opioid use in the last decade, the pain and heartache that comes along with this journey is more out in the open as people are increasingly willing to talk about their experiences. Shea's willingness to share hers exemplifies many family members' bravery and commitment to reducing shame and stigma. Shea steps into the light to share her story with the hope of helping someone else who is lost in the dark.

Why has it taken so long to start this discussion? People who misuse substances in our society (and many others across the world) are highly stigmatized by the cultural narrative about addiction. When you ask people what they think about an "alcoholic" or "addict," they usually mention character and moral flaws, disease, and pessimism about their willingness to change. There is typically disdain for people who lose control of themselves. There is also widespread skepticism about using medication to address the problem, and other beliefs about what people should (or should not) do. Go to rehab, go to a meeting ("just say no!")—areas that have little to no basis in science.

Given this backdrop of stigma and misinformation, when family and friends see signs of substance use by a loved one/a child, they may understandably push aside concerns. The picture of addiction they've been given doesn't seem to fit the individual they love. "He's just experimenting, he'll grow out of it" or "It's just pot" may seem to describe things better than "He has the incurable disease of addiction and we should send him away to rehab." Faced with the stigma of addiction and limited treatment options, it's natural in the short term to say, "It's not that bad" or "What's the big deal? Lots of teens go through a rebellious phase."

However, the data is clear: a pre-teen or teen who smokes tobacco or drinks alcohol is 65 times more likely to move on to marijuana and potentially other substances (NIDA, 1996). And the younger the age of first experimentation, the more at risk a teen is for having serious health consequences down the road (Belcher & Shinitzky, 1998). Teens abuse easily accessible and inexpensive substances like tobacco, alcohol, inhalants like glue or dust-off, marijuana, and the medications found in medicine cabinets like painkillers and anti-anxiety medications. Those who move onto "street drugs" like heroin or cocaine often do so after starting with substances they found in their homes.

Substance use problems are complex and express themselves differently for different people depending on the substance used, the frequency of use, and the amount used, along with other physiological and mental health factors. Additionally, every single struggling person will have a different set of variables that contribute to them changing, or not changing. For example, some teens can smoke pot and drink on the weekends, keep getting good grades, and eventually stop using substances in a problematic way as they take on more life responsibilities. Other teens very quickly become dependent and have problems that may last a lifetime. And still others don't use much, or use infrequently, but suffer significant consequences in terms of their functioning, or alter the course of their life in one bad night (for example, getting sexually assaulted while intoxicated or crashing car while high). Some of these kids will need to go to rehab, others will never get formal treatment and will change for other reasons—reasons such as parental influence, getting a job, or changing their peer group. Some will need to address underlying mental health issues before they can change their substance use. And some will die because they can't or don't change fast enough.

THE IMPACT OF STIGMA

In Shea's painful and poignant description of squishing ants we can see the impact of stigma. The students in her class have absorbed stigmatized views of people with substance use disorders, other mental health issues, and those in the criminal justice system. Our culture includes some extremely sticky beliefs about "addicts": "Addicts lie." "Addicts can't be trusted." "Addicts are powerless to stop their addiction." These blanket statements are not true about every person who struggles with a substance use disorder, and they help perpetuate the myth that there is something "wrong" with people who have substance problems. You don't have to dig very deep to reveal the negative connotations of the word "addict." It implies laziness, a weak will, a failing moral compass, failing at life, being diseased, and it is not uncommon for it to be used as an insult. Listen to the tone of voice that most people use to refer to someone as "an addict" and you will likely hear denigration, suspicion, and judgement.

Why should we care about the impact of stigma? Research has shown that fear of stigma is one of the main reasons people resist seeking help (Copland, J., 1997, Cunningham, J. et al, 1993) and, for those who do seek help, it undermines the quality of care they receive. John Kelly, a psychologist at Massachusetts General Hospital and a leader in the addiction treatment field, in a survey of health professionals who were asked to answer questions about a hypothetical patient, found significantly more negative attitudes and assumptions about a patient referred to as a "substance abuser" than one described as "having a substance use disorder" (Kelly & Westerhoff, 2010). The health professionals were more likely to agree that the "abuser" should be punished for not following a treatment plan and that his or her "character" was to blame. Similarly, studies have found that when treatment providers refer to clients as "alcoholics," they make more negative assumptions such as alcoholics "are liars," "cannot make good decisions for themselves," "have personality deficits that predate drinking," "have spiritual deficits," and "need strong confrontation" (Moyers & Miller, 1993). If you had a problem with substances, would you want the people who are trying to help you to think this way about you? Stigma pushes people away from the help they need and want, compromises treatment professionals' ability to care, and makes generic a problem that is profoundly complex and individual.

Unfortunately, substance use problems often coexist with all sorts of other problems that are also stigmatized, like other psychiatric issues, unemployment, medical, financial, and housing problems, domestic violence, and broken families. People who abuse substances are also likely to be involved in the criminal justice system. Of the 2.3 million people incarcerated in the United States, more than 65% met criteria for a substance use disorder (CASA 2010). In 2016, the most recent date for which federal offense data is available, 47% of sentenced federal prisoners were serving time for a drug offense (Carson 2018). These people are stigmatized for their substance use problem and their history of incarceration. The people who love them, their families, share in all this stigma.

IMPACT ON THE FAMILY

Throughout Shea's story we can see the profound impact Matt's substance use problem was having on his family. There are approximately 21.5 million people in the United States who have substance use disorders (SUDs), including 1.3 million ages 12—17 (SAMHSA, 2014) and for every person with a substance use problem, at least one family member and as many as five other individuals are negatively impacted (Orford et al. 2013; WHO 2014; Daley and Raskin, 1991). Along with millions of Americans like them, Shea, Kelley, Megan, and Larry all suffered (and still do) in many ways, including physical and emotional stress, financial strain (ruin for some), domestic violence, and contact with the criminal justice system and grief.

Family members experience emotions ranging from worry to terror, sadness to hopelessness, disappointment to rage, as well as shame and frustration, or feeling numb. These emotions can be expressed through yelling, begging, crying, or shutting down completely, all of which are understandable reactions and to be expected. No one is born knowing how to deal with a drug or alcohol problem in their family. As Shea notes, "parent does not mean professional."

Shea eloquently describes her initial hopefulness when Matt first started getting treatment, but we can see her anger and frustration build as he continues to struggle, and promises are broken. It is hard to be scared day after day. It makes sense that she is angry that her life is being hijacked by the crises associated with her brother's choices. It makes sense that she is angry at her parents for not being able to fix things. Given her affection for him, it also makes sense she was angry when they did set limits and she felt they were being mean. It makes sense that her parents swung from optimism and hope that treatment had helped their son, to clenched fists and bloodshot eyes while they sat apart on the sofa trying to process what just happened with Matt. And it makes sense that their love for him compelled them to drive hours to visit him in jail and do everything else they could to help him while probably neglecting their own health and each other in the process.

Unfortunately, for a variety of complicated reasons, substance users are at times not motivated to change. In contrast, as Shea describes, their family members are incredibly motivated, and often desperate, for things to change. The predominant messages they receive, however, are to "step away and detach," "do an intervention," and one-size-fits-all platitudes such as "let them hit rock bottom" or "give them some tough love." Families also face a broken treatment system, including lack of access to affordable treatment with professionals trained in effective, evidence-based approaches. Shockingly, health insurance does not cover treatment for family members of the person struggling with addiction.

In culture and in some treatment programs, family members are given the diagnosis "codependence" and told they are powerless to help their loved one and that they need to stop "enabling." All arrows point to "something is wrong with you" and your family, which leads to a reluctance to seek help (Cooper, Corrigan & Watson, 2003), isolation, and further suffering. This is tragic, especially since research has shown repeatedly that family members can help (Smithe & Myers, 2008). If you are a concerned family member, I hope the rest of these segments give you some hope and encouragement to start finding ways to help your loved one, and yourself!

EARLY WARNING SIGNS

As noted, stigma and shame cause many people to hesitate when they start to see changes in someone they love. It is easier to think *they must just be having a bad day, or it's just a phase,* instead of saying, "I'm really scared my child has a drug problem." Parenting a teen or young adult is a tough job on a good day, and the fluctuations of hormones and variations in brain development make figuring out the impact of substances even more complex. Are you seeing a kid crashing from substance use or one that is crashing due to lack of sleep, a wave of hormones, and a fight with a friend? It's a lot to keep track of! But, given the access to drugs and alcohol that children now have at younger and younger ages, it is crucial that parents educate themselves and stay alert.

Shea noticed all sorts of things shift in Matt as he got further into using. His temper, appearance, and engagement with the family and outside interests and friends all changed. As a loved one, you can be on alert for similar changes in behavior or mood. For example, a teen using substances may be more irritable or angry or seem revved up or overly energetic. They may change their routines or friends, like dropping out of sports, struggling in school, hanging out with new crowd, or isolating themselves. They may become more secretive or break more family rules, such as coming home late or cursing. Parents may notice changes in their child's physical appearance, too. Depending on the substance, physical signs also vary.

PHYSICAL SIGNS OF USE:

- Lack of coordination (stumbling, dropping things, staggering).
- Smelling of alcohol, cigarettes, marijuana (other

substances don't typically leave odor).

- Dilated or bloodshot eyes (wearing dark glasses to hide).
- Persistent coughing, clearing throat, or runny nose.
- Change in appearance (loss/gain of weight, poor hygiene).
- Physical injuries or frequent complaints of physical problems (pain, gastro-intestinal problems). Stomach problems (vomiting, nausea, cramps).
- Fatigue, sleepiness.
- Agitation or restlessness.
- Slurred speech.

PERFORMANCE ISSUES:

- Inconsistent performance at work or school (can escalate to complete inability to do the work).
- Lateness, missing things altogether, with poor explanations (or repeated ones).
- Inattentiveness, difficulty following directions, and forgetfulness.
- Pattern of frequent job/school change or unemployment.

BEHAVIORAL SIGNS:

- Sudden changes in behavior including erratic interpersonal style (e.g., swings from compliance to defiance).

- Irresponsible behavior (including cheating, selling drugs, stealing, blaming others for problems, lying).
- Tendency to fight (either verbally or physically).
- Change in friends or social activities.
- Talking about use (may sound boastful).
- Disoriented to time (losing days, inability to explain loss of time, etc.).
- Blackouts.

EMOTIONAL SIGNS:

- Swings in mood.
- Extreme negativism, anger, hostility.
- Reactivity, high emotional sensitivity.
- Nervousness.
- Carelessness, lack of thoughtfulness about the future.
- Depression, withdrawal or seclusion, suicidal thoughts or attempts.
- Defensiveness, paranoia, tendency to argue.
- Apathy and lack of interest or motivation.

TREATMENT

As a clinician, I was tortured throughout the book wondering what advice Matt's parents were getting. Did anyone talk to them about things they could do to set limits and reinforce non-using behaviors? Did anyone teach them ways to engage Matt's motivation to change? What was the aftercare plan for Matt and his family when they left that first wilderness camp? Were his parents educated about reinforcing healthy sober behaviors? Were they educated about the risks Matt faced given his ADHD? Was therapy recommended to help Matt deal with Shea's situation without numbing his feelings? Did anyone check in to see how Shea was doing? So many questions!

We know from Matt's story and many others that rehab is far from a cure-all. For some it is a first step, for others it is not a viable option due to money or life circumstances (e.g., lack of childcare or a job that will not hold if you go away for a month). When it comes to getting help and sustaining change, we also know people need different types of support, at different stages of the change process, including inpatient and outpatient treatment, self-help meetings, treatment for comorbid issues, family therapy, medication, talking to a priest, rabbi, or spiritual leader, starting healthy diet and exercise routines, or picking up a new hobby. A person who is trying to change may need some combination of all these things. The decisions people must make about treatment are complex and depend on what a person has been using, how much, how long, and the underlying reasons for using. Medical and mental health issues, the developmental stage of life, and the supportiveness of the person's environment all need to be considered when thinking through the support plan.

Families of teens who are struggling face particularly tricky decisions and you can see this play out in Shea's story. At first, Matt wanted to be home and his family wanted him there. Being sent away for treatment was traumatic for everyone, including his parents (who most likely did it as a last resort). It is clear, however, that Matt had a difficult time staying sober in his home environment and his friends' accounts of time with him shed light on the difficulties he faced at home. On one hand, Matt's family clearly loved him and wanted to create a home environment that supported him, and we can understand why he would prefer to be "home," where at least some parts of his world felt safe and familiar.

The reality is, however, that Matt's exposure to old friends who were making risky choices, familiar places that were linked with using, and difficult family emotions like distrust, anger, and pressure to be okay could have all added up to cravings and difficulties maintaining the changes he was trying to make. Each person struggling with a substance problem is different. Each family is different. Some people really do need to be in their home environment to make changes, while others need to remove themselves completely. It's crucial that each family dealing with substance problems thinks through the variables that are unique to them. Maybe the home environment is healthy and supportive, but the community around it is problematic. Maybe each family member needs to learn new skills to cope with emotions and communicate before spending time together even makes sense. In any case, when someone is trying to change their relationship with substances, their relationships with the people in their lives must change as well. They may need to end friendships, confront certain relationship dynamics, and make the step of asking for help from strangers whether they be treatment professionals or people they meet in support meetings.

THE IMPORTANCE OF PURPOSE AND COMMUNITY

The most effective treatment strategies and settings focus on all areas of a person's life, not just on helping them decide to use or not. They need new hobbies and interests to compete with using; new friends that share these interests and are supportive of change; and new ways of managing emotions and regulating the body (appetite, sleep, energy). People need understanding and support as they identify their values and senses of purpose and learn to live accordingly. Relationships that may have been damaged will need repair. In many cases, people fall behind in school or at their jobs, and they will need to catch up on lost time. This is all a lot of work, for the person with the problem and everyone trying to help them.

Matt finally seemed to be finding his way when he moved to California, a long way from old triggers to use. There, he connected with a community of people and started to develop his life and sense of purpose without substances. It is tragic beyond words that the court system forced him back to an environment where he was more at risk. These are the goliaths that families face as they try to support their loved one.

THE IMPORTANCE OF FAMILY

And whether the loved one comes home or decides to live in a supportive environment like a sober house, their family needs support. While I don't know what Shea's parents were told, all too often family members are told they must "stop enabling," "distance with love," or "detach" for their loved one to get better. These suggestions are, first, almost impossible to consider when you are a parent concerned about your child and, second, not supported by science. Studies have found again and again that family members can play a crucial role in helping their loved one (Copello et al, 2009, Meyers et al, 1998) and there are skills family members can learn that have been proven in multiple studies to be effective in engaging a substance user in treatment, reducing their use even before they engage in treatment, and improving the overall well-being of the family. There is hope. Keep reading for more on this!

IMPACT OF CO-OCCURRING DISORDERS

Why would it matter if Matt had ADHD? Studies suggest the prevalence of ADHD in adolescents who abuse substances is more than 25% (Oortmerssen, et al, 2012). Teens who struggle with ADHD are prone to taking more risks and making impulsive decisions. They are also more likely to experience difficulties in school and as a result have a shaky self-esteem. They may pull away from other teens who are doing well in school and spend time with teens who are also struggling. Clearly, the best treatment plan for someone like Matt would have to address his ADHD.

While prevalence rates depend on several factors, including gender, age, and type of substances used, studies find that 50% of people with substance problems have other psychiatric issues, including depression, anxiety, and personality disorders (Flynn & Brown, 2008). A large study of the prevalence of co-occurring disorders found that approximately 20% of all people with a current substance use disorder had at least one *non-substance-induced* mood disorder like depression, and 18% had at least one *non-substance-induced* anxiety disorder (Grant et al., 2004). There are also very high rates of Post-Traumatic Stress Disorder (PTSD) and trauma in substance abusing populations (and vice-versa): 29% to 79% of those with PTSD have substance use disorder, while 30% to 60% of substance abusing clients have PTSD (McCauley et al, 2012). This matters because people often turn to substances to self-medicate underlying mental health problems. In the short term, alcohol and cocaine can seem to alleviate depression or social anxiety. Opiates can give people a sense of calm and reduce pain. Substances have effects that people like for some reason (different people, different reasons) and those underlying reasons need to be addressed if you are going to help someone rely less on substances.

Awareness of the importance of co-treating co-occurring disorders is growing, but there continues to be a wide range of provider skill in using evidence-based treatments to address them. If you are looking for treatment for yourself or a loved one, you should ask specifically about the training and the ongoing supervision of the clinical staff when it comes to treating co-occurring disorders.

UNDERSTANDING RELAPSES

"If he doesn't want it yet, he's just not going to be ready to change." On the surface this comment by Matt's counselor makes perfect sense. Matt was relapsing regularly and at that point in the story was not really engaging in his treatment. The counselor speaks to the traditional idea of how a person who abuses substances operates: Matt was a "drug addict" just wanting to use and doing what drug addicts do, which is, supposedly, not take things seriously until they "bottom out" and learn their lesson.

The tragedy in this conceptualization is that it reduces an incredibly complex problem down to one thing, "addiction." Matt was likely seriously depressed and despairing at this point. He was failing his family and himself again and again by relapsing. He started out with poor self-esteem and by this point in his treatment was probably feeling hopeless about his ability to get better. He probably was feeling like he had heard it all, and nothing helped.

Changing a substance problem requires an enormous amount of learning. People use substances for a reason, often multiple reasons. It's a simple idea, but fundamentally important in understanding how to help them. We humans consume many things that have psychoactive properties, meaning they impact our brain and alter our experience in some way. Substances that are typically abused, like alcohol, opiates, cannabis, all tap into the "reward" centers of the brain and affect people in certain ways that they like and want to continue. Drinking, or using any other drug, when you feel anxious is a behavior that is rewarding and then repeated because it works! The drink or drug takes away the anxiety or insecurity. There are reasons people use substances, and they are not crazy, they are rewarding.

Matt was likely using for several reasons, and those reasons likely changed over time. In the beginning, smoking pot and cigarettes could have been a way to bond with friends, escape the stress of his struggles in school, or shut out any confusing feelings he had about Shea's situation. Later, after he experienced the effect of opiates, he had to use to fight off withdrawal symptoms. Using probably also helped him block out feelings of having failed himself and his family by continuing to use. And in the end, he may have been using because it felt better than having cravings, being depressed or suffering from anxiety associated with his experiences in prison or the overdoses of his friends.

Saying Matt simply was not ready to change discounts the reality that he was probably having a hard time managing his cravings to use opioids. Many people, regardless of their substance of choice, experience a strong desire to use, despite their strong desire to make changes. These "cravings" may occur for moments, minutes, or even hours and they may persist for weeks, months, and sometimes even years after last use. Craving can be a response to many triggers such as thoughts, feelings, situations, and people that are associated with using. For example, a person might have a craving if they drive by a place they used to buy drugs, or when they feel "down" or lonely and want their mood to shift.

During the change process, a person needs to learn to cope with triggers and gain confidence that they can tolerate such feelings without turning to use. Over time, cravings will ideally become less frequent and less intense as person develops more competence in not using in response to feeling triggered.

Unfortunately, the pull to use in response to cravings is quite powerful for some. Many people try to cope with urges to use by gritting their teeth and toughing it out, also known as "white-knuckling it." Many people fall prey to the idea that not using is a matter of strength: the stronger they are, the better they'll do, when in fact it has more to do with information, skills, and support. Staying abstinent is a learning process. A person needs to develop behavioral responses other than the drinking or using drugs that they know so well. Using is a known path, tried and true, that requires very little thought. Not using is a new path that requires a lot of thought, effort, and practice.

Matt was probably struggling with all sorts of painful internal experiences that he did not have the skills to manage without using substances. He also started using opioids at a very young age while his brain was still developing, so his cravings for them were most likely significant. It's possible that effective, medication-assisted treatments like Vivitrol or buprenorphine could have given him the space from cravings that he needed while he learned how to cultivate different behaviors and build a healthy life for himself. It's also possible that he just needed an extended time in a sober living situation where he could be out in the world building his life (getting a job, making new friends, engaging in interests) while having a safe, supportive place to come home to each day.

THE SPECIAL CASE OF OPIOIDS

Opioids are substances that come from the opium poppy and include morphine, heroin, and prescribed opiates such as oxycodone, as well as synthetic opioids such as fentanyl. These substances bind to and activate the opioid receptors in the brain, spinal cord, and other organs of our body and in doing so block pain signals sent from the brain to the body and act as depressants to the central nervous system, slowing breathing and causing drowsiness. As a result, they are used regularly in medicine for their analgesic and sedative effects and milder forms help with cough suppression and diarrhea.

They also release large amounts of dopamine throughout the body which causes a euphoric, "feel-good" effect.

Taken for pain relief, opioids can be safe when monitored closely by a trained medical doctor and used for a short time. They can, however, be misused when they are taken in a way or dose other than prescribed and for the effect of getting high. Remember, people take drugs because they have an effect that they like in some way. The fact that opioids decrease pain, both physical and emotional, and can have the effect of making a person feel relaxed and happy makes them compelling to many.

The opioid receptors and neurons in the brain adapt to the repeated use of opioids and users eventually develop tolerance and require higher doses to achieve the same effect. Once someone has become physically dependent on opioids, they will experience withdrawal symptoms when they try to stop using. When the drug is stopped, they have a range of physiological reactions that can be quite severe depending on the length of time someone has been dependent as well as the amount they have been using, including restlessness, anxiety, irritability, muscle and bone pain, insomnia, diarrhea, vomiting, abdominal cramping, runny nose, cold flashes with goosebumps, and involuntary leg movements. All in all, they are pretty uncomfortable, and they happen for anyone (again, to varying degrees) physically dependent on opioids, even chronic pain patients who have been taken them exactly as prescribed. While they may have started out using opioids for an effect like relaxation or pain relief, many people end up continuing to use just so they do not experience withdrawal symptoms.

One key aspect of opioids is that withdrawal from them is, in and of itself, significantly less dangerous than acute intoxication. Opioids affect the central nervous system directly and, in high enough doses, cause respiratory depression and even death. This overdose risk is highest when people with opioid dependence have reduced tolerance after being detoxed from opioids, either through detoxification or incarceration. After a period of abstinence from them, a person's tolerance returns to zero. If they use again, they are at risk for using too much as they often figure, "The last time I got high I needed X amount to feel high, so I should use that much now." That amount with no tolerance floods their central nervous system and they stop breathing: an overdose.

A deadly combination of stigma and antiquated ideas about how to help substance users has contributed to what is now an overdose crisis. In 2015, an estimated 2 million people in the United States suffered from substance use disorders related to prescription opioid pain relievers, and 591,000 suffered from a heroin use disorder (not mutually exclusive) (SAMHSA, 2016).

Drug overdoses are now the leading cause of death for people under 50 years of age, likely exceeding 59,000 in 2016 (Rudd, et al., 2015). These numbers only reflect the loss of individual lives, they do not reflect the terrible impact of loss and trauma on the people who love and possibly depend on them. These numbers are poised to get worse as illicitly manufactured drugs, such as fentanyl, continue to flood the market and show up in cocaine and other drugs of abuse. Since 2008, drugs have been killing more Americans than car crashes (McCarthy & Richter 2016).

Yet despite this crisis, some of the most effective treatments against opioid use disorder are not yet widely used (and even in less use when Matt needed them) because the traditional drug and alcohol treatment industry has been slow to support them. The impact of stigma can be seen in the deep belief that "a drug is a drug" and you don't give "drug addicts" drugs, leading "abstinence- only" programs to reject effective medication-assisted treatment (MAT) as an option for their clients. A 2011 study found that less than 30% of substance use programs offer MATs to their clients (Knudsen, Abraham & Roman, 2011). Another study found that of the 2.5 million Americans 12 years of age or older who abused or were physically dependent on opioids in 2012, fewer than 1 million received MATs (SAMHSA, 2013). According to a recent Pew study, only 23% of publicly funded treatment programs report offering any FDA-approved medications to treat substance use disorders, and less than half of private-sector treatment programs reported that their physicians prescribed FDA-approved medication (Knudsen, Roman, & Oser, 2010).

Shea is right, unfortunately, there have been problems in how these effective medications have been introduced into the market. Research has identified several issues that have contributed to the slow adoption of MAT as an important component of treatment for substance use disorders: lack of well-trained prescribers and poor support for the ones that exist, regulatory policies that restrict the use of MAT, negative attitudes and misunderstanding about the medications among treatment professionals, limits on the dosages that can be prescribed, minimal support for adjunctive behavioral counseling, and the belief that other therapies should be tried first (SAMSHA, 2014). Patients and their families have been exposed to poorly trained treatment providers who themselves hold stigmatized opinions about how best to treat substance use problems and as a result discourage the use of MAT, or prescribe them in ways that make the problem worse. Prescribing too low dosages or encouraging patients to come off them too quickly has been all too common.

At the other end of the spectrum are poorly managed and often unscrupulous clinics that distribute buprenorphine without additional behavior supports or family involvement. Matt tried Suboxone, but he got it from a clinic that his mother, Megan, describes as a "pill mill." Megan insisted she attend the second meeting with Matt. The clinic did not accept insurance and gave out buprenorphine after a urinalysis and a ten minute visit with a doctor who she recognized as an OB/GYN she called on four years prior as a surgical rep! The clinic did not offer the additional therapeutic supports and monitoring that people typically need in order to use the medication effectively. Matt's efforts with the treatment were abruptly ceased by Megan when she realized Matt was only taking a half a film so that he could have six left at the end of the month to sell for $20 a strip. Thankfully, government agencies have recognized the terrible outcomes associated with these clinics and many states in the country are starting to put stricter regulatory mechanism in place.

MEDICATION-ASSISTED TREATMENT (MAT)

As Shea's story moves along I felt like pulling my hair out for them because Matt and his family did not have the benefit of access to (or health professionals failed to connect them with) several effective medications that help opioid users sustain changes. Shea wonders how many times someone relapses before it is simply a return to using. I wonder how Matt would have responded on Vivitrol, a medication that could have helped him maintain abstinence from opioids by blocking their euphoric effects and thus making them less appealing. Or maybe he should have been on a therapeutic dose of buprenorphine, but monitored closely by an attentive board certified addiction psychiatrist.

Medication-assisted treatment (MAT) is an evidence-based approach that combines the use of medications with counseling and behavioral strategies. Like most, if not all, medications, those appropriate for treating substance use disorders have their downsides and side effects, but the evidence supporting them as effective agents against relapse and overdose death is robust. The data suggest as many as 90% of people detoxed completely off opioids relapse within the first one to two months unless treated with these medications (Smythe, et. al, 2010). Other research has shown that these medications double the rates of abstinence from opioids when compared to placebo or no medication (Connery, 2015).

Buprenorphine, which is a partial opioid agonist, activates opioid receptors in the brain but does not produce the maximal effects that full opioid agonists, like heroin, do. It does not incite feelings of euphoria, but it produces enough effects to trick the brain into thinking it is receiving a full agonist. Consequently, buprenorphine reduces cravings for opioids and provides relief from withdrawal symptoms. It is protective in lowering overdose risk as it blocks the receptor sites in the brain that opiates would otherwise attach to. Buprenorphine is taken once a day, in pill form, and because its half-life is longer than the opioids people misuse, it frees people from the trap of constantly thinking about their next high, allowing them to think about other interests and get on with their lives. Many people may decide to stay on the medication indefinitely as coming off feels like it puts them too at risk for relapse. For others, the dosage is gradually tapered off over time, giving the person time to learn to live without opioids without being derailed by cravings. Unlike methadone, buprenorphine can be prescribed by specially trained physicians in a doctor's office and does not require one to attend a methadone clinic.

Naltrexone is a medication taken in pill form daily that blocks opioids from binding with the opioid receptors in the brain, thereby eliminating any sense of a high. The effects last one to two days. It is often tried before committing to the long lasting, extended-release injectable version called Vivitrol in order to assess for tolerability and side effects. Vivitrol is a once-monthly intramuscular injection (like a flu shot). Naltrexone is not as effective as Vivitrol for preventing relapse since one can easily stop taking it and quickly be unblocked.

Methadone is a full opioid agonist that, like buprenorphine, has a longer half-life than the opiates that people commonly misuse. Administered in a methadone clinic, this medication reduces or eliminates cravings and reduces the need to use other opiates.

PREVENTING OVERDOSE

Until very recently, most treatment providers were in denial about the need to prepare families for the risk of opioid overdose. And many still don't. If you or someone you love has ever struggled with an opioid use disorder, it is wise to be prepared in the case of an overdose. The opioid users most at risk for overdose include people who inject opioids, people who use in higher doses or in combination with other sedating substances like alcohol or benzodiazepines, and people who have recently detoxed from opioids. Others at risk include people who have sexually transmitted diseases such as HIV, liver or lung disease, or conditions such as depression.

Narcan (naloxone) is a medication that can save the life of someone beginning to overdose from opioid use. It works by causing the opioids in a person's system to eject themselves off of their receptor sites in the brain, in other words reversing the effect of the opioids, and thus prevents the central nervous system from shutting down. It is important to note this reversal effect is temporary and depending on the type and amount of opioids consumed a person may needed repeated doses of naloxone. For this reason, even if the person wakes up and seems better it is essential to call 9-1-1 immediately after administering a dose of naloxone for an overdose, so that you can also get professional medical care.

Narcan (naloxone) is available upon request without a prescription in many states from participating pharmacies. If you or someone you live with is at risk of opioid overdose, it can be life-saving to have Narcan on hand and to be trained in how to administer it.

IMPACT OF SHAME

Here I want to make a special point about shame. As we have discussed, substance use and other mental health disorders are stigmatized conditions. Studies have found that people who struggle with these problems are judged to be dangerous, blameworthy, infuriating, and repellent (Corrigan et al 2006, Angermeyer et al 2004), weak, incompetent (Rusch et al. 2005), responsible for their disorder (Corrigan et al. 1999) and unworthy of help (Corrigan, Watson and Miller 2006). They experience these judgements and feel shame. No one wants to be addicted to drugs or alcohol.

For most parents, their children are an extension of their heart and soul, so no wonder they also suffer from the shame of stigma. Studies have found that they are blamed as the cause of the problem, or the reason the problem is not resolving (Corrigan & Miller 2004; McCann & Lubman 2018). They are labeled with the "disease of codependency" (a diagnosis that is not supported by the American Psychiatric Association), feel ashamed of this label, and they feel ashamed of their child (Larson & Corrigan 2008, Corrigan et al, 2006). This all translates to enormous amounts of shame and self-blame. A survey of over 600 parents who had a child with an emotional or behavioral problem found that 72% of parents blamed themselves, often all the time, for causing their child's problem (Eaton et al., 2016).

Parents and other family members commonly feel guilty about things said out of anger or confusion (e.g., "I can't believe you are a drug addict!" or "You are a disgrace to this family."). They second guess themselves about how things were handled (e.g., "I wasn't around enough" or "I was too hard on him… I didn't know he was depressed") and for decisions that were made along the way (e.g., letting drug use go unaddressed early on). These difficult thoughts and feelings can lead to a desire to isolate or withdraw from others, efforts to make up for errors by being "perfect," or a tendency to blame others for the problem.

WHAT CAN FAMILIES DO?

As they look for help, family members are flooded with suggestions from well-intentioned loved ones and professionals. People have strong opinions about what to do with someone misusing substances and unfortunately many of them are antiquated ideas, colored by stigma and not supported by research. Additionally, unethical and even dangerous treatment providers have proliferated in the current opioid crisis. Parents are told that their child "needs to hit bottom" and "there is nothing you can do" or "he needs to go to rehab"; treatment brokers get paid for referring to specific programs, regardless of the needs of the client they are referring. These programs want access to the insurance benefits even if they don't provide all the services an individual may need (like effectively treating co-occurring conditions); there are countless stories of people being kicked out of treatment the second their benefits run out, with no planning for what to do when this happens.

UNDERSTAND THE UNIQUENESS OF YOUR FAMILY & YOUR CHILD

The truth is, there are many positive pathways to change, and understanding the uniqueness of your child and family increases the likelihood of success. Certainly, you may have things in common with other families dealing with substance problems, but understanding your child and situation really does help. The reality is there is not one easy answer or one best approach to fixing the situation. Substance problems are typically incredibly complex, and each person has different reasons for using, different things that will help them to stop using, and different variables that will contribute to them finding their motivation to change.

It's understandable that black-and-white, all-or-nothing advice can feel powerful as it would seem to fix the problem quickly, once and for all. The one thing, however, that has been demonstrated over and over is that considering various options, and being willing to allow multiple choices, is a powerful way to help. If you can understand that one size doesn't fit everyone, it will give your loved one or child breathing room and help them feel like they are part of the decision. And these two things will make it more likely they will buy into some plan for change.

EDUCATE YOURSELF ON WHAT YOU CAN DO

Contrary to the traditional belief that there is nothing you can do for a loved one using substances, there are a variety of very effective, research supported strategies that families can learn. You can *stay involved* with your loved one, you can *influence them* positively to change, and you can learn to *take care of yourself*. And your loved one can change. It just might not be the straight march towards health that you pray for, so educating yourself about the problem and ways to address it, learning skills to positively reinforce change and set limits around substance-using behaviors, and taking care of yourself throughout is crucial to long-term success.

The effective strategies you can learn have been shown again and again in research studies to be effective in engaging people in treatment, reducing their substance use before they enter treatment, and improving the overall well-being of the family—all good outcomes! The Community Reinforcement and Family Training approach (CRAFT) is a behavioral and motivational treatment for families (Smith & Meyers 2008) and has been developed and researched in randomized controlled trials. CRAFT is a set of skills family members can learn that help them support non-using, positive behaviors by noticing, praising, and rewarding (called "reinforcing") them. These are the behaviors you would like to see more of, like abstaining from substance use, and they include behaviors that directly "compete" with substance use, like going to the gym, getting a job, or engaging with new friends. In CRAFT, families also learn how to NOT reinforce destructive (substance using) behaviors, the ones that you no longer want to see.

If you have been taught that any involvement on your part will only make things worse ("enabling"), it's important to clarify what enabling is and what it isn't. In our culture, there are many ideas about substance problems that are meant to help people understand things better, but often have the unintended consequences of making people feel worse about themselves and more confused. The concept of "enabling" is most definitely one of these. Many parents feel like anything they do to help their child is enabling, but that could not be further from the truth.

Enabling is acting in ways that reinforce or support (unintentionally) substance use or other negative behaviors. Examples include covering for your loved one's absences from work or school or giving them money to help them get by when you know they have run out due to their use. Usually these choices come from an understandable desire to saw off the rough edges for your loved one, a very natural impulse, but one that prevents your loved one from learning the naturally occurring outcomes of their own choices and actions.

On the other hand, actively reinforcing positive behaviors or helping your loved one engage in behaviors that compete with using is not enabling. For instance, paying for treatment when your loved one is asking for help or cooking your loved one dinner and watching a movie they like when they have decided to come home sober are all actions that reinforce non-using behaviors.

Given the terrible emotional strain family members are under much of the time, it's not uncommon for people to make threats ("I'm going to kick you out" or "You are cut off") that prove too hard or extreme to follow through. This is sometimes called enabling, when it is actually just an example of desperate emotions running the show rather than acting from a clear plan that has been discussed in advance. Many family members also have a hard time figuring out when to reward sober behavior. Matt's parents bought him that new motorcycle because he was sober at the time and they wanted to give him something to feel good about while he waited for legal issues to pass. The timing of the reward may have been too soon, before he had enough other sober, non-using behaviors in place, like a job. It could also be that Matt needed the experience of working and saving more of his own money towards the bike in order for his self-esteem to really start to mend. But his parents wanted to give him experiences of happiness, as any parent with a suffering child would, and so they may not regret using that opportunity.

There were not enough examples in Shea's account for me to determine if her parents were "enabling" him or not. Unfortunately, it's a word that gets tossed

around a lot when things simply aren't working, and
we need someone to blame. I would argue that many
of Matt's parents' decisions and actions were just efforts
to help their son, in any way they knew how, with the
information and skills they had at the time. And as was
the case with Matt's parents, after three failed attempts
in treatment programs, when Matt said, "If I had this
bike, I would ride cross country and have something I
enjoy more than drugs," they were desperate to support
it as it seemed like a way out of the hell they were all in.

UNDERSTAND THE PROBLEM

One of the first things you can do as you try to help is
to understand the "function" of the person's use. When
you understand the function of someone's use, it also
helps you realize that using drugs or alcohol has some
positive effect for them. It might not be your cup of tea
or a need you feel, but it means something to your loved
one, otherwise they wouldn't be doing it! You may be
surprised by the powerful, measurable effects of a soft-
sounding thing like "understanding"!

First, identifying what is reinforcing about using
a substance can point you in the direction of other
avenues of reward. What does your loved one get from
the substance? Do they use it to manage social anxiety,
boredom, or attention problems? Do they use it to

avoid emotional pain or insecurity? If you understand the purpose substance use serves—what is "reinforcing" or "rewarding" about it—you can help the person learn other coping skills and rewarding behaviors so that they don't turn to substances. Look for experiences that have similar benefits, that can compete with substances and take over the role they are playing. Consider people, situations, and activities that lower anxiety, bring pleasure, and lift self-esteem.

Second, understanding what your loved one is getting from using will help you see patterns and some predictability in a situation that has probably felt out of control. While it won't take it away completely, this can help you feel less anxiety which will help you problem-solve more effectively. Your loved one's behavior will seem less random and you can strategize to intervene in ways that make sense.

Finally, understanding that there are reasons for a behavior has another important effect: it helps increase your empathy for the person who is doing it. I'm sure I don't have to tell you that empathy can be hard to muster sometimes! Knowing that a person's decision to use is partly about their struggle with anxiety, or depression, or feeling part of the group, can go a long way towards empathizing with them and wanting to help. It can also help you to not take their choices around substance use so personally, which families tend to experience as a conflict diffuser and huge relief. This increased empathy and decreased tension will improve the chances of better collaboration all around.

LET NATURALLY OCCURRING CONSEQUENCES PLAY A ROLE

Finding a way to make life as positive as possible when your loved one is not using can do a lot to compete with the "positive" effects of substances for your loved one. At the same time, they need to experience the negative consequences that are a direct result of their actions or choices. This is the real-world voting on your loved one's behavior. Do their choices get them what they want or not? When they can't get out of bed in the morning, do they miss class and have to speak with the principal? When they show up late for work, do they get written up and threatened with job loss?

There is an abundance of research that shows people really do start to change when the outcome of their actions is not pleasant or enjoyable for them. Allowing for naturally occurring negative consequences to happen is one way to allow that process to happen. Unfortunately, many family members end up making themselves the "negative consequence." As they buffer or protect their loved one from the outcome of their choices (like getting them cleaned up and into bed instead of leaving them passed out in their clothes on the floor), their loved one never experiences any of the natural outcomes of their behavior (like waking up on the floor in puke-caked clothes). Instead, they have a partner or parent expressing lots of upset and anger, in addition to lecturing and trying to control the situation. The outcome is that your loved one doesn't really learn how the larger world feels or reacts to their decisions. Instead, they think you are the problem…"My mom is a nag and a drama queen" or "My dad is such a control freak." They don't make the link between their actions and real-world outcomes. They may also turn to substances to help tune you out or block any feelings they have about your reactions. This does not put blame on the upset family member, it simply describes a common response that leads to the exact behavior you are hoping to reduce.

It is important to note that there are some consequences you can't allow, like letting a loved one drive drunk instead of figuring out other transportation, for instance. It is also important to think through any consequences that will result in a backlash towards you that you should not or cannot tolerate due to safety. Take some time to examine the potential consequences and decide what you can tolerate.

The main thing is to assess whether you are reflexively

protecting your loved one from the reality of how their choices play out in the real world, which interferes with learning and growing. Your job is to figure out which negative consequences will speak for themselves, which of these you can live with, and then get out of the way.

HELPING YOURSELF HELPS

Behavior change is not a sprint, it is a marathon over hilly, rocky terrain, sometimes while being buffeted by hurricane winds. The strain of watching your loved one struggle to change and oftentimes being on the receiving end of their failures (verbal aggression, physical violence, theft, etc.) can push you to a very dark place.

While it is normal for family members to think they will feel better once their loved one is doing better, neglecting your health and other areas of your life until then has all sorts of negative outcomes. When you are not eating well, not getting enough sleep, and don't have any healthy outlets like exercise or hobbies, you are more at risk for being reactive, anxious, and easily frustrated just at the time when your family needs you to be strong, calm, and optimistic. When you don't tend to your other relationships, they start to fall apart and become another source of strain, not something you need. You may be so focused on your loved one who is struggling that you pull away from friends and other sources of support.

Many people end up isolated and quite alone with their heartache. To be an effective helper, you need to channel some of the time and energy you spend worrying about your loved one back into yourself and your other relationships. This will leave you better equipped to manage the pain and upset you are likely experiencing.

And let's go back to the impact of shame, which can make it very difficult to open up about what you are dealing with. Maybe you are worried about gossip or exposure in your community. Maybe you're an "I don't ask for help" kind of person or are just flat-out embarrassed by the problem. These reactions are all understandable, but not so helpful!

Why? Because withdrawing from other people and outside supports takes a toll. Trying to handle stress alone can put you at greater risk for depression, anxiety, fatigue, and despair. It decreases your resilience and hurts your ability to roll with the punches and be effective. Social support, on the other hand, has been shown to do just the opposite: it improves mood, lowers anxiety, and makes you more resilient. Last, social support can expose you to new options and avenues for change. While each family situation is unique, the support you can get from family, friends, professionals, and other parents who have gone through similar struggles can be crucial to helping you help your child.

Shea's story all too clearly shows how one person's behavior choices can upset the entire family apple cart. Her parents were in pain and fighting with each other and agonizing over different opinions about how to approach the problem. His sister Kelley was in New York City worrying from afar, and along with Shea was in pain too. Missing their brother, mad at their brother, mad at their parents, feeling sad for their parents, and this all went on for years and maybe sometimes still does. The miles her parents put on the car, driving to check on Matt. The sleepless nights, the constant worry and disagreements, being distracted and unable to focus on school or work. The sole focus on whether a loved one is doing drugs, or not, can deplete an entire family system.

One of the powerful things about Al-Anon (or Narc-Anon) is the message that taking care of yourself really matters. Self-care is also one of the main components of CRAFT, because research has shown how crucial it is for family members to experience joy, relief, rest, and comfort while you go through the storm with your loved one using substances.

UNDERSTAND THE TREATMENT OPTIONS

As I've said, there are many more treatment and support options to explore other than "rehab" and twelve-step groups, and having options to choose from is a key to motivating change. With your loved one's situation in mind, do your homework and be an educated consumer. Know your options, and if you are seeking treatment, ask how the treatment providers are trained and supervised. Are they experts in treatment strategies supported by science? Do they support the use of MATs? Do they include you as a family member?

END

I am honored to have been asked to write a few things to support Shea's efforts to bring Matt's story out in the open. Shea is one of hundreds of thousands of people in this country who have lost a loved one to a drug overdose. As their children have been dying, parents have become increasingly vocal and united in their efforts to change our culture and the treatment system so that people stop dying and get the help they need. Shea's story sheds light on the experience of a sibling, who lost her playmate, hero, protector, teaser, companion, and confidant. Her adored brother. The most powerful part of her story for me is her ability to channel the love she and the rest of his family felt for Matt despite all that they went through as he struggled with his addiction to drugs. They never stopped loving him and obviously still do, as Kelley encourages her to "remember the good, the normal," all the things that were Matt beyond his addiction.

Everything we know from research and clinical experience points to this: families matter the most in this fight. In fact, *family* is the leading reason people seek help for substance problems, and family is the force that sustains change once help is found. We know families are endlessly dedicated to loving and helping their struggling loved ones. But we also know that they get virtually no help themselves, and that they suffer greatly. It can be stressful, maddening, and terrifying to love someone dealing with a substance problem. This pain is compounded with the burdens of shame, isolation, and silence. And in their silence, we are losing perhaps our most powerful resource and agent of change.

Thankfully, people get better. I see it happen all day long in my work with people who struggled with their use of substances. I also have the honor of working with their families, who also get better. People can learn skills and can change their lives. In part because of the great courage of advocates like Shea and her family, I hope you can see that there is great hope. Treatment can help. Understanding the root of the problem and learning skills to cope with underlying issues can help. Changing the environment can help. Positive reinforcement from friends and family can help. Learning from real world, natural consequences can help. Learning to talk about the problem and reduce shame and defensiveness can help. Finding a sense of purpose can help.

Know that you can make a difference with your loved one. It is not always a straight and smooth path, but it can be a more hopeful, sane, and doable path, with better outcomes, when all parties involved learn new ways of coping and interacting with each other.

CMC: Foundation for Change (CMC:FFC) has the singular goal of getting effective and accessible evidence-based tools to the families of those struggling with substances. We train parents in the Invitation to Change Approach which draws from the most effective strategies found in 3 evidence-based treatments: CRAFT (Community Reinforcement and Family Training), Motivational Interviewing (MI), and ACT (Acceptance and Commitment Therapy). Put simply, the Invitation to Change Approach brings science and kindness together: evidence-based strategies are combined with compassion and care, making a wealth of research-supported and clinically tested knowledge accessible, practical, and understandable. We help parents support one another as well as their children. We want to change the conversation from one of shame, secrecy, and suffering to one of pride and hope. CMC: FFC does not provide treatment. Our goals are to build and maintain a national peer-to-peer parent coaching program in collaboration with The Partnership for Drug-Free Kids, to partner with community-based organizations to develop the resources and infrastructure they need to implement self-sustaining support systems and to develop a comprehensive online presence for sharing resources, building community, and connecting families to support.

For more information on how you can support our work please visit www.cmcffc.org/donate

REFERENCES

Angermeyer M C, Matschinger H, Corrigan P W (2004) Familiarity with mental illness and social distance from people with schizophrenia and major depression. Schizophrenia Research 69(2):175—182

Belcher H M, Shinitzky H E. (1998). Substance Abuse in Children. *Archives of Pediatrics & Adolescent Medicine, 152*(10).

Bureau of Justice Statistics Home page. (n.d.). Retrieved from https://www.bjs.gov/index.cfm?...

Carson A E (2018) Prisoners in 2016 Washington, DC. US Dept of Justice Bureau of Justice Statistics, NCJ251149, p 13 https://wwwbjsgov/indexcfm?

CASA Columbia (2010). Behind bars II. Center on Addiction and Substance Abuse (CASA) https://www.centeronaddiction.org/addiction-research/reports/behind-bars-ii-substance-abuse-and-america%E2%80%99s-prison-population.

Connery H S (2015). Medication-Assisted Treatment of Opioid Use Disorder. *Harvard Review of Psychiatry, 23*(2), 63-75.

Cooper A E, Corrigan P W, Watson A C. (2003). Mental Illness Stigma And Care Seeking. *The Journal of Nervous and Mental Disease, 191*(5), 339-341.

Copeland J (1997, 04). A qualitative study of barriers to formal treatment among women who self-managed change in addictive behaviours. *Journal of Substance Abuse Treatment, 14*(2), 183-

190.

Copello A, Templeton L, Powell J (2009). *Adult family members and carers of dependent drug users: Prevalence, social cost, resource savings and treatment responses.* The UK Drug Policy Commission.

Corrigan P, Miller F (2004) Shame, blame, and contamination. J of Mental Health 13(6):537-548

Corrigan P, Watson A, Miller F (2006) Blame, shame, and contamination. J Fam Psych 20(2): 239—246

Corrigan P W, River L P, Lundin R K et al (1999) Predictors of participation in campaigns against mental illness stigma. J Nervous and Mental Disease 187(6):378—380

Cunningham J A, Sobell L C, Sobell M B, Agrawal S, Toneatto T (1993). Barriers to treatment: Why alcohol and drug abusers delay or never seek treatment. *Addictive Behaviors, 18*(3), 347-353.

Daley D C, Raskin M S (1991). *Treating the chemically dependent and their families.* Sage.

Eaton K, Ohan J, Stritzke W et al (2016) Failing to meet the good parent ideal. J Child Fam Stud 25(10):3109—23

Flynn P M, Brown B S (2008, 01). Co-occurring disorders in substance abuse treatment: Issues and prospects. *Journal of Substance Abuse Treatment, 34*(1), 36-47.

Grant B F, Stinson F S, Dawson D A, Chou S P, Dufour M C, Compton W, Kaplan K (2004). Prevalence and Co-occurrence of Substance Use Disorders and Independent Mood and Anxiety Disorders. *Archives of General Psychiatry, 61*(8), 807.

Kelly J F, Westerhoff C M (2010). Does it matter how we refer to individuals with substance-related conditions? A randomized study of two commonly used terms. *International Journal of*

Drug Policy, 21(3), 202-207.

Knudsen H K, Abraham A J,Roman P M (2011). Adoption and Implementation of Medications in Addiction Treatment Programs. *Journal of Addiction Medicine, 5*(1), 21-27.

Knudsen H K, Roman P M, Oser C B (2010). Facilitating Factors and Barriers to the Use of Medications in Publicly Funded Addiction Treatment Organizations. *Journal of Addiction Medicine, 4*(2), 99-107.

Larson J, Corrigan P (2008) The stigma of families with mental illness. Academic Psych 32(2):87—91.

McCann T V, Lubman D (2018) Stigma experience of families supporting an adult member with substance misuse. Int J Mental Health 27:693—701

McCarthy N, Richter F (2016, November 18). Infographic: Drugs Are Killing More Americans Than Road Crashes. Retrieved from https://www.statista.com/chart/6805/drugs-are-killing-more-americans-than-road-crashes/

Mccauley J L, Killeen T, Gros D F, Brady K T, Back S E (2012). Posttraumatic Stress Disorder and Co-Occurring Substance Use Disorders: Advances in Assessment and Treatment. *Clinical Psychology: Science and Practice, 19*(3), 283-304.

Meyers R J, Miller W R, Hill D E, Tonigan J (1998). Community reinforcement and family training (CRAFT): Engaging unmotivated drug users in treatment. *Journal of Substance Abuse, 10*(3), 291-308.

Moyers T B, Miller W R (1993). Therapists' conceptualizations of alcoholism: Measurement and implications for treatment decisions. *Psychology of Addictive Behaviors, 7*(4), 238-245.

New NIDA Report Summarizes Data on Drug Use Among

Racial and Ethnic Minorities. (1996). *PsycEXTRA Dataset.* doi:10.1037/e313802004-006

Oortmerssen K V, Glind G V, Brink W V, Smit F, Crunelle C L, Swets M, Schoevers R A (2012). Prevalence of attention-deficit hyperactivity disorder in substance use disorder patients: A meta-analysis and meta-regression analysis. *Drug and Alcohol Dependence, 122*(1-2), 11-19.

Orford J, Velleman R, Natera G, Templeton L, Copello A (2013). Addiction in the family is a major but neglected contributor to the global burden of adult ill-health. *Social Science & Medicine, 78*, 70-77.

Rudd R A, Seth P, David F, Scholl L (2016). Increases in drug and opioid-involved overdose deaths—United States, 2010-2015. *MMWR Morb Mortal Wkly Rep.* 65(5051):1445-1452.

Rüsch N, Angermeyer M C, Corrigan P W (2005) Mental illness stigma. European Psych 20(8):529—539

Smith J E, Milford J L, Meyers R J (2004). CRA and CRAFT: Behavioral approaches to treating substance-abusing individuals. *The Behavior Analyst Today, 5*(4), 391-403.

Smith J E, Meyers R J (2008). *Motivating substance abusers to enter treatment: Working with family members.* The Guilford Press.

Smyth B P, Barry J, Keenan E, Ducray K (2010). Lapse and relapse following inpatient treatment of opiate dependence.2010 *Irish Medical Journal.* Jun;103(6):176-9.

Substance Abuse. (1998). *Jama, 279*(10), 802.

Substance Abuse and Mental Health Services Administration (SAMHSA) (2013). Results from the 2012 National Survey on Drug Use and Health: Summary of National Findings, NSDUH Series H-46, HHS Publication No. (SMA) 13-4795. Rockville,

MD.

Substance Abuse and Mental Health Services Administration (SAMHSA) (2014). https://www.samhsa.gov/data/sites/default/files/NSDUH-FRR1-2014/NSDUH-FRR1-2014.pdf

Substance Abuse and Mental Health Services Administration (SAMHSA) (2016). Center for Behavioral Health Statistics and Quality (CBHSQ). *2015 National Survey on Drug Use and Health: Detailed Tables*. Rockville, MD.

World Health Organization (WHO) (2014) Global status report on alcohol and health. http://apps.who.int/iris/bitstream/handle/10665/112736/9789240692763_eng.

ABOUT THE AUTHOR

S.C. Megale was born in 1995 near the Manassas battlefields. She is a novelist, humanitarian, and student of the University of Virginia. Her first published novel, *This is Not a Love Scene*, saw a 2019 release with St. Martin's Press/Wednesday Books, and her projects have been profiled by USA Today, CBS News, The Washington Post, and more. She was diagnosed with a neuromuscular disease shortly after birth confining her to a motorized wheelchair, but not to the soil – her travels and work have carried her to Europe, Oceania, and unnumbered off road adventures. A storyteller with fourteen completed manuscripts, her writing is both emotional and frank. Megale is the younger sister of Matthew Joseph Megale (1990-2017), the subject of this book.

Made in the USA
Columbia, SC
07 December 2019